TO:

....

FROM:

....

DATE:

....

MADE NEW

52 DEVOTIONS FOR CATHOLIC WOMEN

NELL O'LEARY, LEANA BOWLER, BRITTANY CALAVITTA, JENNA GUIZAR, AND LIZ KELLY

THOMAS NELSON
Since 1798

This book is dedicated to every woman in the Blessed is She community. We wrote this book for you. The Lord is making us new.

Made New

© 2021 Blessed is She®, Inc.

Project director: Jenna Guizar
Project manager and editor; questions and scripture selection: Nell O'Leary, JD
Theological editor: Susanna Spencer, MA in Theology

Published in Nashville, Tennessee, by Thomas Nelson. Thomas Nelson is a registered trademark of HarperCollins Christian Publishing, Inc.

Thomas Nelson titles may be purchased in bulk for educational, business, fund-raising, or sales promotional use. For information, please email SpecialMarkets@ThomasNelson.com.

Scripture quotations are taken from New Revised Standard Version Bible: Catholic Edition. Copyright © 1989, 1993 National Council of the Churches of Christ in the United States of America. Used by permission. All rights reserved worldwide.

Any internet addresses, phone numbers, or company or product information printed in this book are offered as a resource and are not intended in any way to be or to imply an endorsement by Thomas Nelson, nor does Thomas Nelson vouch for the existence, content, or services of these sites, phone numbers, companies, or products beyond the life of this book.

Cover design and original artwork: ash ulmer design
Interior design: Emily Ghattas

ISBN 978-1-4002-3027-3 (audiobook)
ISBN 978-1-4002-3025-9 (eBook)
ISBN 978-1-4002-3024-2 (HC)

Printed in China

21 22 23 24 25 DSC 10 9 8 7 6 5 4 3 2 1

CONTENTS

Part 3: Beloved

Part 4: Believing

Part 5: Becoming

INTRO

By Jenna Guizar

I have always struggled to get into a groove with my prayer life. I have wondered when the Lord would make a way for me to commit to prayer and be disciplined in it for longer than two weeks. He has yet to come through. In all reality, I'm the one who needs to make the time and commit to actually *doing* it. You may know this struggle too.

When I carve out prayer time in my calendar, commit to it in my heart, and take the first step of doing it, He pours out His grace for me to respond. Once I have taken each step of coming closer to His heart, it is in His heart where I find my home. I find a Father who longs for me, who loves me, who accepts me as I am, and at the same time calls me to more.

I invite you to journey with me, dear sister, to walk through the next fifty-two weeks as we rediscover our value, our worth, and our identity in Our Lord's eyes. He is waiting for you and me, and He desires to be in relationship with us. All it takes is a response to His call: *yes.*

Blessed is She is a community of women who desire to grow in their Catholic faith through prayer and community. The authors—Nell O'Leary, Brittany Calavitta, Leana Bowler, myself, and Liz Kelly—share stories in individual sections focused on five different themes of our identity (beheld, belong, beloved, believing, and becoming). Within each section, the writer walks through ten different phases of life, writing a weekly reflection centered around a scripture verse. We include two reflection questions for you to sit with each week as a way for you to find takeaways and lessons for your own life. We hope the Holy Spirit moves you to sense His promptings on your heart.

PART 1

BEHELD

by Nell O'Leary

Set aside the myth that your value as a woman is contingent upon what you do, how you accomplish, or how you perform. Instead, accept this invitation from the Lord to fully embrace your identity and worth as being made in His image and likeness. You are utterly beheld in His loving gaze.

We walk through eleven stories from my life, eleven unique stages from early childhood through adolescence to mature adulthood, which are paired with illuminating scripture passages. We encourage you to open your Bible and follow along. Take time with the questions and let them sit inside your heart.

He called a child. Matthew 18:2

WEEK 1

MY WORTH AS A CHILD
Childhood

Extended family dinners at our dining room table all sounded the same. Dishes clanged up against the glass cups close to one another as we filled out the table's added leaves. The dining room was situated in a quiet, dark side of the house facing the driveway with one long, lone, locked window. Adults talked about everything under the sun, embracing that old adage that "children are to be seen and not heard," and we complied.

Meanwhile, my aunts and uncles opened their voices over politics, religion, you name it. My grandfather's oxygen tank tube for his emphysema whipped around as he gestured wildly. My mom stepped in and out of the kitchen through the swinging door to check on dessert. My dad cleared his throat as his in-laws waged verbal war upon one another.

I knew we were not present in the conversation, we five kids. We didn't have a place to agree or disagree, even as we aged. We only had a place of silence.

My parents divorced when I was seven, and meals around the dining room table were replaced with stacks of all five kids' papers, my mom's own schoolwork, and place mats that needed to be wiped down from microwaved fettuccine Alfredo splatter.

I have thought a lot about what it meant to be welcomed as a child. The unique identity of being made in God's image and likeness. The space a child holds in a family, a family as boisterous as mine. The belonging of the lonely child, the welcome of the sad one.

I thought I was a good and welcomed child based on my behavior. That my being loved by God was dependent on how quietly I could dangle my legs off those brocade chairs, how I could enjoy yams without enough brown sugar, no complaints. I thought God was handing out a behavior grade, and His approval of me depended on earning an A.

It took years to unravel this narrative that children were meant to be neither seen nor heard based on the premise that there wasn't much to see or hear in kids. We were to be well-behaved, a good reflection on our upbringing, and not an embarrassment to our parents.

Now, maybe that dining room table had a lot more wiggle room than I remember. But you probably have your own version of this from childhood: an instance when your lovability was reduced to the number of your years, your lack of sophistication, or an assumption that you had nothing to offer. It could have come in the form of an unpleasant teacher or a challenging stepparent who would have preferred you weren't around.

I invite you to walk with me back through the looking glass into that memory. In your replay, speak the words of Our Lord to that difficult adult from your past: "Whoever welcomes one such child in my name welcomes me" (Matthew 18:5). Jesus insists you're worthy of welcome because He comes right along with you. We matter enough to hold space, be it silent or raucous, even as children.

As we meditate on today's scripture selection, sit with Jesus' discussion of being humble like a child. Perhaps when He speaks of this,

He's talking about that essence of humility that children possess: seeing ourselves as we truly are. The appearance of being well-mannered isn't the same as having a happy heart. To draw close to Him and His Sacred, Holy Heart is to trust that His love for us makes us intrinsically lovable. And when we can release our own narrative of our position in God's eyes being based on a performance grade, we can really enter into His kingdom.

And do you believe it, sister? Do you believe that the vulnerable, tenderhearted, maybe steel-faced and young you can and should be welcomed? All the times we heard that we were too much, too loud, too big, or maybe, conversely, too meek, too soft-spoken, too shrimpy, we heard we were not welcome.

But that is not Jesus' way. His way welcomes us as we are and invites us to more.

READING: MATTHEW 18:1–5

- What does feeling welcomed mean for you? Name a time you've been welcomed or when you've welcomed someone else, whether as a child or as an adult.
- If you're stuck on performing well to earn approval, examine that. Can you release it in your relationship with your loving and nurturing Father? If this isn't your struggle, pray for someone in your life for whom it is.

Forgive
each other.

Colossians 3:13

WEEK 2
CHOOSING
FORGIVENESS
Sisterhood

I gasped and stumbled in circles with my arms above my head, hoping to breathe again after my track race. The 300-meter hurdles had never been my strong suit, and this race in particular had been brutally embarrassing. My knee was bleeding from my fall in the last hundred meters, and my pride was hoping for air along with my lungs—as everyone, including a friend-turned-enemy ("frenemy"), had witnessed my sister running along the track on the inside, shouting encouragements at me as I limped across the finish line.

This was to be my sister's last track meet of her senior year, and in her event later that afternoon, she won first place. I rushed to celebrate with her, trying to avoid that "frenemy," but upon seeing her, my heart contracted. She had no words for me, as she usually didn't, preferring to bypass me for my older, cooler sister. In that moment, I turned uncomfortably away from her to face my sister, waiting to be passed over by both of them, waiting for inevitable rejection.

My sister nodded at this girl, moving past her smiles to me. She clutched my hand and swung it up in the air, as if we had landed on the Olympic podium together. "Wahoooooo!" she shouted. "We finished the year strong!"

I whooped too, cheering for her, for me, for our sisterhood, for our last shared year of high school. My heart cheered because my sister had chosen me to celebrate with. In front of her friends, the frenemy's friends, and my friends, all of God's creation, she chose me.

Have you ever been the one who isn't chosen? Isn't chosen for a team, for a bridal party, for a trusted secret, for a roommate, for a friendship? In the intricate relationships of our lives, especially those tightly woven tapestries of female friendships and sisterhood, rejection is the tug that unravels our own self-worth.

And these feelings of being passed by or passed over can build one upon the other until we find ourselves the resigned victim, griping about perpetual wounds. I have been tempted to accept and believe that no one would want to choose me anyway. I'm not "enough"— you name it—clever enough, funny enough, smart enough, mature enough, experienced enough. And my deepest desire to be beheld as a sister you'd *want* to pick may have been fulfilled in that instance at the track meet, but it didn't convince me to be confident for the next round.

My lack of trust in my value was all tied up with desiring a particular outcome, not in accepting what came my way.

And the frenemy? The easy target of my resentment and complaint? I suppose it's easier to villainize her than to bear with her. Saint Paul reminds us in today's scripture for reflection, Colossians 3:13, to do just that: to bear with the people we have complaints against. This girl's choice of my sister over me didn't have to dictate my self-perception.

We get to choose to forgive—not to ignore the complaint, but not to soak in the sorrow of rejection either. Saint Paul calls us to "forgive each other" (Colossians 3:13). My sister's big, bold move of celebrating our sisterhood instead of shutting me out was a healing moment. It gave me the strength to forgive, trust, and hope again.

You are called to the same, sister. In the small slights and in the big ones, Jesus calls us right up to Himself to remember we are always chosen by Him. And in the confidence of being perpetually His choice, perhaps we can extend the grace to forgive those who couldn't or wouldn't choose us. It was never about them anyway.

READING: COLOSSIANS 3:12–14

- Have you faced repeated rejection from a friend? Have you experienced the healing love of sisterhood and forgiveness despite this? Think of your own story here.
- Jesus always chooses us, regardless of who else does. Remind yourself of this today. If someone in your life could use attention and being "chosen" or included, reach out to her.

◇

Do not neglect the gift that is in you. 1Timothy 4:14

WEEK 3

SETTING ASIDE PEER EXPECTATIONS

Young Adulthood

The first leg of our high school choir tour was a Catholic church for its evening Mass on a Saturday in Arkansas after a twelve-hour bus ride. My fellow sophomores shuffled past the holy water font into the choral pews up near the altar, elbowing and jostling each other.

It dawned on me that I didn't actually know how many of them were Catholic; our school wasn't religious, and on Ash Wednesday my siblings and I were the only ones with ashes on our foreheads. So, I hastily dipped into the holy water, made the Sign of the Cross, and then genuflected before I quickly scooted into the pew.

My friend next to me asked, "What was up with that?" I just shrugged it off before we rose to begin one of the few hymns in our repertoire.

When it came time to kneel for the consecration, the girl to the right of me was leaning forward with the kneeler up, talking to the guy a row ahead. My neck burned with that buzz of embarrassment as I slid off the pew and onto my knees on the stone floor. I clutched my eyes shut.

But as I started down the aisle to receive Holy Communion, I saw a senior from the tenor section line up too. Then two soprano junior girls. A handful of chaperones. All walking up to receive Jesus in the Blessed Sacrament.

The small things—the genuflecting and kneeling, the Sign of the Cross, the praying along with the responses—had felt like big things. A small choice could have big consequences, i.e., people thinking I was stupid or weird. And when you're a teen or young adult, even the smallest disapproval from your peers can decimate you.

This is something we hope to mature out of, but it's hard to balance our choices against other people's expectations, even as adults. If anything, at this point, I've piled everything together into one big expectation jumble. The boundary between where my stance on a topic ends and my perceived reaction to that stance by my peers begins to blur at times. Instead of shedding others' expectations, I'll slip into them faster than I did that pew after my hasty genuflection. To fit in, I'm supposed to look a certain way and act a certain way to avoid judgmental reactions in real life or on social media.

And for you, sister? Are you waiting for external validation to be different? Avoiding the risk of people not liking who you are, living caged by your own fears of not being accepted? When circumstances arise and you are faced with the seemingly little thing that is maybe a big thing, what steers you? Is it a desire to be yourself? Is it a desire to blend in? Is it anxiety over being a disquieting mirror to others?

Living out my faith made me uncomfortable then, and sometimes it does now too. I didn't want to "set the believers an example in speech and conduct" (1 Timothy 4:12).

I wanted what we all want on some level: to be both accepted and affirmed without taking any risks, to steer safely past standing out while feeling assured that people like you because you don't make them uncomfortable.

Pray with this advice from Saint Paul: "Do not neglect the gift that is in [us]" (v. 14). This gift of the Holy Spirit in us through the sacraments is one we should tend and allow to bloom within our lives. Release yourself, slide onto your knees, set aside fear today. We are given the gift of the Spirit by a loving Father, and we are likable and accepted eternally by Him.

Devoting ourselves to the practice of leading by example in speech and conduct is both a little thing and a big one. We start out with the small decision to pray grace before meals in public and build up to inviting a neighbor to Christmas Mass. God is calling you to share your faith.

You never know *who* will be encouraged by your (embarrassed or imperfect) example.

READING: 1 TIMOTHY 4:12–15

- Is Jesus nudging your heart to push past some insecurities and share your faith by example? Is He asking you to let go of the lie that you won't be accepted for who you are?
- List off two ways you can respond in charity if someone thinks your faith is weird. Remind yourself that your identity does not hinge on his or her acceptance of you, but on God's infinite love of you.

"The Spirit of truth will guide you into all the truth." John 16:13

WEEK 4
BREAKUP AND DAMAGED HEARTS
Rite of Passage

H e's not the one for you." My mom's words went slow-motion into one ear before they hit my brain. I looked up at the ceiling of the hip restaurant to see a bronzed bull poised to fight. I looked down at my hands, nails half–torn off from enduring the finals of my first year of law school. Finally, I looked across the table at her.

It all came rushing forward: How much I wanted to prove to my family I could date the "right" guy after my college fiasco of a boyfriend. How hard I wanted to pick a "nice" guy so I would believe I was a "nice" girl.

I choked out, "I'm sorry I let you all down." She hurried over to my side of the booth, and everything came out. How unhappy my family had seen me, despite my covering it up with glowing updates and cute photos. She rubbed my back as I shared the harder, darker parts of my relationship.

I could hardly bear to hear the truth, but I also needed permission to examine reality. My dating history was short and full of teenaged drama that deeply eroded my sense of identity and how God saw me.

And when I had shared with my then-boyfriend about my past relationship, my mistakes and wounds, I had been judged and belittled by him. He was unable to value my journey with its imperfections. I was simply damaged goods to him, and I let him treat me like that because I thought I deserved it. I allowed him to assign my identity to me.

The ensuing months post–break up were brutal, but exactly the emotional rite of passage I had to go through to move beyond depending on a guy to affirm my value as a child of God. The truth spoken by my mom, siblings, and friends was guided by the Holy Spirit. I could hear it only with the grace His truth brings. Each of us can only process and examine transitions in maturity with the generosity of God's patience for us.

I stepped away from my comfortable habit of dating someone who needed me and who propped up my ego. Any time we shed a cozy, safe habit, we get a chance to make a new one. And my new one was to say in those sad, lonely moments when I wanted a guy to make me feel better, *Jesus, I love You. Jesus, I trust in You.* When I ached for the old comforts, I reached to this new one. That was and is my leap of faith.

If a leap of faith feels impossible, and mine did, I recommend starting with little steps of faith. I trusted Jesus would carry me from that moment to the next, and I set aside the fear that the next day I would wake up just as nauseated by my circumstances as when I fell asleep. Truth can hit hard and hurt.

In your life, perhaps someone has spoken this truth to you: a truth that you knew, that you avoided, that you didn't think you could even cope with if it hit you squarely in the face. And you get to take the gift of that truth, even if "you cannot bear [it] now" (John 16:12), collapse over it, and rise back up, steadied by the Spirit. No, none of us are "strong enough" to make it through this transition by ourselves. We desperately need God and the people He works through.

Pray with today's scripture selection: "When the Spirit of truth comes, he will guide you into all the truth" (v. 13). We don't and can't always come to it on our own. Isn't it a relief that not every truth-seeking mission is all on you? That a new season of maturity will be illuminated by the Holy Spirit?

The Lord has bestowed a new worth on us through His love for us. He has sent His Holy Spirit to guide us, to "declare to [us] the things that are to come" (v. 13). Whatever you leave behind as you transition—the sad cloud of a boyfriend, a thankless boundaryless friendship, an emotionally draining work environment—you get to step into a new habit, one rooted in the truth that your identity comes from Him. Nothing and no one can shake that.

READING: JOHN 16:12–15

- Where have you experienced a big shift, transition, or "rite of passage"? Take the time to ask God to walk with you through the memory of it.
- Have you experienced someone sharing a hard truth with you? Or have you been the one to share the hard truth? What graces were present as it played out?

"Each tree is known by its own fruit." Luke 6:44

WEEK 5
THE FRUITS OF
MY FAILURE
School

I moved my pencil over the paper slowly and deliberately, as though I understood the complexities and nuances of my Advanced Placement Calculus exam problem. I erased, muttered, and sketched out the problem. I used the techniques my patient teacher had taught me: break a problem down into parts and approach each part as an individual puzzle. On that fifth question on the final page, I drew my face closer to the answer section and began writing.

It was an apology note to my grader. This person was probably some underpaid teacher's assistant who loved math and would be the one to face the graveyard of math dreams that was my test.

No, I didn't pass the AP exam, and, yes, I had to take college math the following fall because I didn't receive the credit. I knew that would happen before I even left the testing center. I knew it while my friends were excitedly consulting each other on what they got for each question in the testing center lobby while we waited for the elevator. I knew that I was the one who probably shouldn't have been in AP Calculus to begin with.

Over that summer, I never answered my friends' phone calls about my celebration plans for when the AP exam results came back.

When we gathered for our senior midsummer bonfire and people boasted about which college classes they would skip out on, I fell silent.

You see, I took the failure of this test, the failure of my ability to even *finish* this test, to demonstrate that I was a fraud, a rather stupid person surrounded by clever and hardworking friends. Not only was I an imposter, but I must be a lazy one. Despite tutoring sessions with that saintly teacher, the formulas and equations had floundered around in my brain with nowhere to lodge.

I kept thinking of myself as a bad tree bearing bad fruit like in today's scripture: "Nor again does a bad tree bear good fruit; for each tree is known by its own fruit" (Luke 6:43–44). If I were a good tree, I would have borne academic success. I'd be known by my fruits as the one who not only tried hard, but was good at what she tried hard at. Not the one who tried *really* hard only to land on her face. I had missed the entire point that the fruits are spiritual, not accomplishments or accolades.

Have you tried hard, sister? Have you tried hard and cared about something, a relationship, a test, a job, a spiritual habit, and still felt like you failed? You've probably had something in your life like my AP exam. And if you're anything like me, you may have concluded that you would rather hide from your failure than face it because facing it would mean that it defined you. Instead of being a person who tried and didn't succeed, you would be the person who wasn't good enough in the first place.

We often tend to evaluate our external successes and failures as if they define us. But these lessons in failure for me were actually an invitation to examine the spiritual fruits in my life. Where was God calling me to practice charity, patience, and kindness toward people struggling in my life, even when that person was *me*?

When we step back to examine what it means to be "the good person out of the good treasure of the heart produc[ing] good" (v. 45), we can rediscover what "good" means. Being good means being of God and close to Him, partaking and sharing His love. We are "good" when we listen to His promptings and accept His grace to act well. Partaking in the life of the Divine through the sacraments helps us produce and harvest those good fruits.

Our Lord tells us in Luke's Gospel, "It is out of the abundance of the heart that the mouth speaks" (v. 45). Be fair-minded, sister. Look at the totality of your circumstances. Set aside the perceived failures or successes and think about your heart, because those fruits are lasting and the ones that really count.

READING: LUKE 6:43–45

- Have educational decisions been a point of stress in your sense of your true identity as God's child, whether that's not as much education as others around you or degrees you aren't "using" in your particular season of life?
- Before labeling yourself based on your failures, take a good look at the fruits of your heart. List for yourself the fruits of love you've witnessed blooming there.

Let us make humankind in our image. Genesis 1:26

✾ WEEK 6 ✾

EXPECTATIONS OF
THE FAMILY LABEL
Family of Origin

I stacked more blocks for my three-year-old, partly to hide myself in anticipation of the mounting tension in our family discussion. I peeked out from behind them to gauge how fast the fight would break out. I figured it would ramp up as my brother weighed in on whether or not college would be worth it in the future, if education as a whole had completely relinquished its call to educate children nowadays, and whether or not the country was going to hell in a handbasket.

We were on a family-wide vacation at the beach, eleven grandkids, our parents, siblings, and spouses. We are spread out over the East Coast and Midwest, so coming together once a year was quite the feat. But the real feat was getting through a visit without too many dropped expectations, hurt feelings, or blowups. We both loved and disagreed fiercely. Such was the story of our big Irish-Catholic family.

I interjected, "We all have valid points in this conversation so there's no need to raise our voices." I should have known that would be gasoline on the fire. Someone stalked off the sun porch, in-laws were suddenly busy checking their phones, and I made a mental note to stop running interference.

In most families, someone takes on the peacemaker role. And, in our family, that had been my role for many years. Any conflict situation posed a test for how I could draw opposing family members back together. My ears had one setting: listen to mitigate damage.

My family spans the spectrums from atheist to spiritual to devout Catholic, and then from dyed-in-the-wool progressives to even-more-dyed-in-the-wool conservatives. But from a young age onward, I wanted nothing more than to keep the peace and keep the relationships alive, at just about any cost, including that of my own mental health and emotional boundaries.

I took pride in being the one people came to with any size quibble. Even when he or she didn't ask for a mediator, I took it upon myself to advocate. You may identify with a different role inside your family of origin, and maybe your identity also has been wrapped up in this role, difficult to untangle and yet begrudgingly held close.

Sitting there on the porch, I was struck by the opportunity to relearn this truth: my lovability in my family does not depend on my skillful de-escalation of tempers.

We are made in God's image and likeness as we read in today's scripture selection, Genesis 1:26. Each of us individually reveals God in our own unique way. We are different, brilliant, and necessary for the whole Mystical Body of Christ. We are meant to be ourselves, and this truth is unchangeable.

And yet every single one of us also reflects how we were raised. These imperfect people we love, and maybe disagree with vehemently, impress and shape our sense of identity. That impact sometimes strengthens, or lessens, our trust in our truest identity as beloved daughters of our Divine Father.

It can be easier to cling to the incomplete versions of our own story, measuring our identity up against how we're doing in that story, but often neglecting the larger narrative of God's truth in our lives as we read in today's scripture.

It can be a challenge to set new habits that reorient ourselves in the light of God's view on our identity. And yet here it is, so clearly stated at the moment of creation: "Then God said, 'Let us make humankind in our image, according to our likeness'" (Genesis 1:26).

Does this bold declaration that you are made in the very image and likeness of our Creator God give you joy? Or maybe a little trepidation to give up the comfortable script of your own label or your family's?

God is calling you to wholeness and an abiding assurance. Step with confidence into this identity, into this unshakable measure of your value as His creation and the identity He bestows on you with His love.

READING: GENESIS 1:26–27

- Is there a narrative of your role or identity in your family of origin that you'd like to reassess as an adult? How can you take steps toward that today?
- How does this call to remember you are made in God's own image and likeness affect your own story? What would you celebrate or change about your approach?

"Love one another as I have loved you."

John 15:12

WEEK 7
INVISIBLE UNMET EXPECTATIONS
Friendship

I hovered over my phone before sending the text message: "If you're around, any chance you could grab a few things from the store? We're sick. Anthony is out of town."

I leaned back against my daughter's unicorn headboard. She sat up to cough again, deeper. I could hear my oldest coughing from his room, and the baby began his own bark-coughing across the hall. Swinging my feet over the edge of the bed, I found my way to the medicine cabinet. I grabbed the thermometer and headed to the baby's room.

High fevers all the way around, coughs, borderline croup, and my head was spinning. I counted the days until my husband would return from his trip.

I had reached out to a close friend, thinking a rotisserie chicken, jug of orange juice, and some applesauce would do the trick. I had tried my mom and my older sister, but they were sick too. I was sure my friend would help.

"Ah! I am meeting a friend for lunch and then picking someone up from the airport later. So sorry! Maybe tomorrow night? Or Monday morning?" I read her text and leaned back again, and this time just cried.

I had always been a love-with-never-saying-no kind of friend. Boundaries in friendship didn't exist for me. Maybe it was being a Midwesterner who was raised to think saying *no* was a rude response to any request. Maybe it was being someone whose close friends growing up said *no* to her a lot. Maybe it was being focused on being the best kind of friend possible.

So when my friend said, "Not right now," I took it personally and to heart. My immediate reaction was that she wasn't a *real* friend. But the more thought-out response was that her boundary was simply different than mine.

And months later, we took the time to talk face-to-face. It turned out I too had let her down many invisible times. My life was a bit of a circus; I'd had three kids in four years while she was working long hours, dating, and constantly rearranging our plans because of my ever-changing schedule.

It was a mistake to measure our friendship by one incident instead of the totality of the many years we had been close. I also assumed I had been the only one giving. We can be so blinded by our tally board, keeping track of the times we've picked up the phone for them, or met them out at an inconvenient location, that we miss out on all that we have received.

I gave and gave, but I also counted and counted. I realized my hidden motivation: seeking her affirmation of my lovability.

Today's scripture selection is intense. "No one has greater love than this, to lay down one's life for one's friends" (John 15:13). Laying down your life doesn't always mean literally dying for your friends. It also can mean loving without counting, giving without seeking the comfort of affirmation that you're *the best* at being a friend, trying to show them God's love instead of impressing upon them how wonderful you are.

These little moments when we're stung by a friend can be a gift, a tiny insight into how and why we operate the way we do in friendship. What motivates you in a friendship? Is it guilt, comparison, or a hankering for affirmation? Maybe it's a blend along with genuinely wanting to give when you see someone in need. Maybe this is a time to reflect on what healthy, boundaried, but also no-strings-attached love in friendship looks like.

When Jesus invited His apostles to "love one another as I have loved you" (v. 12), we receive a great insight into what His love looked like in friendship. And this love is shown in all the stories of how Jesus treated His apostles and disciples throughout the Gospels. He gave from a secure place of knowing who He was. He gave relentlessly without counting the cost. He gave Himself as a gift because He had true awareness of His worth and identity in the Father.

He wants this freedom in friendship for us too, sister.

READING: JOHN 15:12–13, 17

- Have your expectations not been met by a friend? What happened and how did you reconcile, if you were able to?
- When you pray about loving your friends like Jesus did, what would that look like practically for you? What would you change about your relationships now?

"Do whatever he tells you."

John 2:5

WEEK 8
TRUST IN
UNFORCED LOVE
Romantic Relationship

I rolled over on the futon away from my fiancé. My frustration overflowed over whose parents would pay for the alcohol at our wedding reception. I was beyond irritated and contemplated if I should start crying. I could go either way. I rolled back to face him as he sat against the wall on my apartment's carpeted floor.

I chose the rage rainstorm. "How could you not want to hear my perspective? Is this how it will always be? You not listening to what's important to me?" He stared blankly at me, exhaustion crisscrossing his face.

We had been in the weeds of wedding planning for most of his trip out to visit me during his last year in law school. The red-eye flight between finals had seemed like a good idea to escape the Michigan snow and enjoy the Vegas warmth, but he was probably rethinking that.

I gave myself over to tears. I partially knew this would force his hand to be the one to reach out because I was the (very) wounded party. The other part of my cryfest was the sheer exhaustion of living three time zones apart and remote planning a wedding in the zone sandwiched in between.

We eventually figured out the reception. And over a dozen years of marriage later, I have also figured out that emotional manipulation, no matter how effective in the short-term, leaves long-term resentment and builds awful communication habits. I had been operating this way out of a combination of learned behavior and doing whatever it took to get to my desired outcome.

In the beginning, I struggled to trust that my husband would love me if I didn't force him to. And without his agreement, his approval, his assent, I struggled to see how anyone would love me.

The tears-for-results approach shut out my husband of decision-making, messed up emotional intimacy, and showed my meager trust in the communication process. We had to disagree openly, talk through our perspectives, and try to land on a compromise in order to grow in our relationship.

Also, disagreement did not mean that he did not value me enough to agree with me. I learned to untether his love for me from his catering to me. He could, did, and does love me *and* disagrees with me.

Maybe for you, this lesson has come in a family relationship or an opinionated boss. Disagreement does not mean death by disapproval. Sometimes we have to work through the problem while being open to the possibility of not getting our planned outcome. That can be a challenge in trust.

In today's scripture for reflection, we ponder how the Blessed Virgin Mary, our heavenly Mother, approached her Son, Jesus, at the wedding feast of Cana, and said: "Do whatever he tells you" (John 2:5). She didn't lay the guilt on her Son to make water into wine right then under the threat of tears. She trusted that He would take care of the situation that she had pointed out: they needed more of something.

She simply said, "They have no wine" (v. 3). He did challenge her, "Woman, what concern is that to you and to me? My hour has not yet come" (v. 4), while He still paid attention to the problem at hand.

He will pay attention to our relationship problems too.

A note for all my sisters who feel like the road to marriage is experiencing too many detours: have you been able to trust that Jesus will lead you to a person who is a good fit for you, one who will help you grow in holiness and deepen your capacity for love? Jesus is available to us even when we disagree with where He's taking us.

Jesus wants to perform miracles in our lives, miracles of healing our scars, restoring trust in Him and each other, rebuilding how we think and speak about and to our loved ones, and releasing us from the grip of fear. He broke me free from my fear of losing control, and He has taught me to trust that He desires to help me, as He does you.

Let Jesus remind you that He loves you and wants to help you. Let Him teach you how to ask, trust, and let go of what happens.

READING: JOHN 2:3–11

- How is the health of your closest relationship? Do you find yourself relying on emotional manipulations to force specific results? Or are you feeling like you're on the other end of games?
- Jesus wants you to trust and be able to freely love in your relationship. How can you invite His example of love into your life? Take this to Him in Adoration or when you're next at Mass.

"I will give you rest."

Matthew 11:28

WEEK 9
DEFINED BY OUR SUCCESSES
Workplace

I sat in a stark cubicle holding a book of the criminal rules of procedure on my lap. My husband texted to check in on my first day at my new position. "It's great!" I texted back. I set my phone down and swallowed hard.

My boss was kind in allowing me to learn the ropes. It was an unpaid role, but he treated me with the respect of a colleague. The other attorneys were mostly generous with their knowledge. I was fully licensed. I had clerked for a federal judge. I had served as Managing Editor of the Law Review. My student note had been published. But those credentials didn't matter after the job market had crashed.

Job listings typically calling for one to three years of experience jumped up to five or more. I landed a few interviews, but no one would hire me.

Maybe instead of spending my second summer working abroad as a consultant to the European Union, I could have worked harder to get a local firm internship. It occurred to me that instead of building community at school, I could have locked myself in the law library and studied harder.

And yet, years later, after being a stay-at-home mom, I slowly grew into my role as Managing Editor for Blessed is She alongside Jenna Guizar. I had no idea that I would find just the right way to use the gifts I'd been given after feeling like a failed attorney. It has been an expectation shift of what "success" looks like.

As women, we can carry the emotional weight of our work around our necks. We may have expectations that just aren't met in our working lives. Even if it's a difficult cohort, a terrible economy, or just the bad luck of the draw, somehow we find a way to blame ourselves. Maybe you also think you could do more and therefore "be" better.

Do we let our work define us? I'm talking about successes and failures, valleys and mountains. Is our identity tied up in our performance? Even when that performance may be evaluated out of our control: the boss who is racist or sexist, the intense hours that blur our work-life boundaries, the subtle discriminations based on our Catholic faith. Is what we do, and how well others think we do it, becoming who we are?

I had to unpack this notion that I was my credentials, that I was my accolades. I look back at this time of humility and know that I needed it for a reason. I needed to be held by the Lord and told I was loved because of who I was, not what I did. Our abilities will fluctuate throughout the years. It's wearying to constantly hinge our sense of who we really are upon what we're doing today.

Let us set it all down to rest with today's scripture for reflection. Jesus invites us to come to Him for rest, those who are "weary and are carrying heavy burdens" (Matthew 11:28). He doesn't encourage us to come to Him for a to-do list or a pep talk on how to lean in. He doesn't say that He will teach us how to maximize our time and leverage our workflow.

He promises we will "find rest" for our souls (v. 29). He offers us His yoke, to share in His work alongside Him. Maybe instead of burying ourselves in productivity, we can step back into the identity we're given by God as His precious daughters whom He has called to do His work here on earth.

And that work? It may not be flashy. It is simple and humble: sharing the gospel through living a life of faith, hope, and love. We can integrate the gospel into our daily work whether at home, in the clinic, or in the office. If we're "failing" at excelling in the workplace based on a perception of what we "should" be achieving, but we're loving those around us, we're succeeding at the *real* work. This is true even if the failures at work blind us to the value we are given by God's love.

Living a gospel life is the kind of work we can't wear out from, because in that gospel work Jesus' rest awaits us. He awaits to fill us up to the brim and fuel us with His love.

READING: MATTHEW 11:28–30

- Do you revolve your identity around what you do during the day for work? How can you recenter it on your identity as God's daughter?
- Do you regularly feel like a failure because of how you spend your time? Jesus is calling us to a life of heroic virtue and living out the gospel. Now focus on improving *that* job.

✦

Let us
consider how
to provoke
one another
to l ove and
good deeds.

Hebrews 10:24

WEEK 10

DESPERATE FOR COMMUNITY

Church Community

L ook," I hissed to my husband as Mass wrapped up. "They have their kids too. Okay, go for it." While I should have been praying, I was making spatial calculations. *If we leave the pew now, we should arrive in the back at the same time as them.*

We had a toddler and an even smaller toddler. We had no couple friends. And since I had stopped working and was at home full-time, I was desperate for friends. So we had been observing this couple for a few months at Mass. She had a cute, dark pixie cut and always wore interesting earrings. They seemed to have two boys, but I couldn't be sure because some Sundays they had two boys with them, sometimes only one.

That fateful Sunday morning, the stars aligned. My husband and I were both there with both our kids, and they were both there with both their kids. We caught up to them just before they started down the church steps.

"Well, hi there!" I chirped and tapped the mom's shoulder. "Your kids were so well-behaved! What's the secret?" She responded wryly, and our families stepped away from the busy doors to talk. We discovered mutual friends and that our oldest boy and their second oldest were the same age. We exchanged numbers. I practically floated to the car. Couple friends! Finally! Maybe!

Maybe your parish community is booming with activities and ministries. Or it could be that you have few opportunities to connect with other Catholic women in your area. That was the case for me. Despite growing up at the parish and coming back to be married and have our babies baptized there, meeting others was rare at our commuter parish, aside from practically jumping strangers in the back of the church.

My longing to be supported by other Catholic women stemmed from having no reinforcements in living out my Catholic faith. I had found some community on the internet with other Catholic mom bloggers, but so many of the women I knew in person thought I was, well, crazy. Crazy for leaving my career as an attorney before it had taken off. Crazy for having kids close together (and no plans to stop). Crazy for not immersing myself in pop culture. I needed to share these struggles with other Catholic women to make sure I wasn't *actually* crazy.

And yet even in our parishes, we can feel so separated, like there isn't a place for us given our season of life: being single, struggling with fertility issues, divorced, at-home with a brood of kids, or a full-time working mom. Maybe to create that space of belonging, you can take the leap and approach a stranger after Mass. My own leap has brought us close friends who encourage us greatly and bless us abundantly.

When we sit with today's scripture reflection from Hebrews, we are reminded to encourage one another. Saint Paul wants us to think about ways we can "provoke one another to love and good deeds" (Hebrews 10:24). Those deeds might start small, a rosary group, a text thread of prayer requests, a brunch invitation. But God can do so much with the little seeds we plant.

Love in friendship starts as a small, fragile plant, needing lots of sun, rain, and encouragement. Relationships are often slow to grow on the surface, but those deep roots are what keep them upright. And we need relationships in our church community, especially as women.

Remember that God is in relationship: Father, Son, and Holy Spirit, and we are made in His image and likeness. We need so desperately to lift each other up, to remind each other that we're not crazy for being Catholic in a sometimes crazy world. We need to encourage each other to pursue the gifts God has given us and to hold each other in prayer.

Saint Paul urges us to not be "neglecting to meet together" (v. 25). So, reach out of your comfort zone, tap that woman on the shoulder, and build some community together. We need each other to grow in our identities as beloved daughters of God.

READING: HEBREWS 10:24–25

- What is lacking in your community life as a Catholic? Where can you find ways to build up, encourage, and gather together with other women?
- If you have a vibrant community, consider how open you are to welcoming new members. In what ways can you invite or seek out women who may feel they aren't included?

"Everyone who believes in him may not perish but may have eternal life."

John 3:16

WEEK 11

LET IN THE LORD'S LOVE

Relationship with the Lord

Making my way along the back wall of the retreat's auditorium, I bounced the baby on my hip. She wasn't *my* baby. My three babies were at home, devouring hot dogs and playing board games with my husband. I was in Phoenix helping my colleagues facilitate a Blessed is She women's retreat. This baby's mom needed a break to listen to a speaker, and, as part of the hospitality team, I swooped in.

As I walked, pausing periodically to check if she was asleep in my arms yet, I half-listened to the speaker, Beth Davis. She shared how transformed God wanted each of us to be. I peeked at the baby again for sleepy eyes. What the speaker said sounded great. And I noted the women nodding along. As the child in my arms surrendered to sleep, I took a breath to listen, this time with my heart.

I wasn't sure that I believed the speaker. I mean, I believed this was true for *her* experience. But mine was more of an I-said-my-prayers and I-get-a-good-grade kind of deal. As she encouraged the ladies to ask God what He wanted to tell them, I resisted.

I knew He wanted me to make good choices and to generally behave. Besides, if I asked and He spoke something more into my heart, I wasn't sure I could handle anything more piled on my to-do list. I didn't really want to hear it.

This question is a challenge for each of us. *What do You want to tell me, Lord?* He speaks through intermediaries like speakers at a retreat, scripture verses that pop into our minds, the promptings of the inner voice of our hearts, a song lyric that comes across our screen, a friend's heartfelt social media share, a quiet sunrise.

But we may not ask Him what it is that He wants to tell us because we can anticipate the response, or so we think.

I thought to myself that hot afternoon, *What do You want to tell me, Lord? Have I displeased You? Have I not done enough? Am I not a good daughter?* And what I felt in my heart were the words, "Let Me love you."

It wasn't an audible voice or a parting of the heavens with a beam of light. It was the slow unearthing of what I had known and He helped reveal to me: I had held my heart away from God.

I held Him far enough away for me to be in control, steady, and safe. I earnestly prayed and had for years. I frequented the sacraments. My husband had helped me flourish immensely in my spiritual life through our shared worship and how we raised our little family.

But yet this obstacle of feeling as though I was lacking held me back. In my pride, I wanted to present myself to God as completely pieced together and deserving of His love. Maybe you've felt undeserving too, sister.

Of course, none of us are worthy of His love on our own. None of us can earn today's scripture meditation: "For God so loved the world that he gave his only Son, so that everyone who believes in him may not perish but may have eternal life" (John 3:16).

Love is always a gift. Our personhood is a gift, given to us by a Father who loves us beyond imagination. We don't earn it by crossing i's and dotting t's on our spiritual to-do list, just in case you're also tempted to believe that. We let it grow within us as we stay close to God through the sacraments and a life of prayer.

Saint John tells us, "God did not send the Son into the world to condemn the world" (v. 17). God the grade-distributor, God the evaluator, God the counter-of-my-points is a god of my fears. The God we believe in loved us into creation and sent His only Son, "in order that the world might be saved through him" (v. 17). He came to offer salvation to you and to me.

Accept His love for you, sister. Today, tomorrow, and the next day. You were created for this: to know, to love, and to serve God in this world and, in the next, to experience the eternal happiness of God's love.

READING: JOHN 3:16–17

- Does the idea of letting God love you make you uncomfortable? How aware are you of His immense love for you?
- Think of a woman in your life who needs to know how lovable God has made her. Share your journey through this identity with her today.

PART 2

BELONG

by Brittany Calavitta

Set aside the myth that your approval as a woman depends on how others see you. Instead, embrace that you belong to God's family and that belonging is a gift He won't rescind. Accept this invitation from the Lord to fully embrace your identity and worth as being made in His image and likeness. You completely belong to a loving and attentive Father.

We walk through ten stories from my life, ten unique stages from early childhood through adolescence to mature adulthood, which are paired with illuminating scripture passages. We encourage you to open your Bible and follow along. Take time with the questions and let them sit inside your heart.

Beloved, we are God's children now. 1 John 3:2

WEEK 12
DISCOUNTED LOVE
IN THE DARKNESS
Childhood

My father had a darkness in him I never could quite grasp. But, then again, I suppose a three-year-old isn't equipped to grasp that sort of thing anyway. A three-year-old is naïve to the weightiness of the world, powerless against the collapse of family structures, cycles of abuse, or mental health disorders.

I felt powerless against his drug addiction. "It was the cocaine," my mother would tell me. That was the darkness that haunted my father. It was the darkness that compelled him to hide hypodermic needles in our planters and to stay out late in the moon-soaked night to feed his shadows.

And his darkness, it haunted me too. It hovered over me through their divorce, his ensuing absence, and all the questions it left in my sullied heart. As the years whirled on, I often found myself wondering about him, this stranger who shared my name. I wondered who, where, and how he was. But mostly, I wondered why holding on to drugs was better than holding on to his daughter.

And somewhere along the line, all of the wondering about him got me wondering about me. The questions usually came with big heaves filled with feelings of worthlessness. Who could love me if I could not have been loved even by my own father? Who would rally for me, pick up my broken pieces, and carry me to safety?

The answers to those questions did not come right away. No, the answers to those questions had to be discovered through a series of mistakes, of looking for light in places that only fed the darkness. And so I clawed my way through the shadows of anorexia and bad relationships until I discovered Him—the One True Light.

Today's scripture says, "See what love the Father has given us, that we should be called children of God" (1 John 3:1).

I often wonder about this love spoken about by Saint John. That's where we usually veer. It's easy to read about God's love for us—to flip through the pages about Christ's death and resurrection or to skim the promises about our place in the story of eternity. But it's also so easy to discount it. It's easy to look up from the tattered pages of our Bibles and see only the flaws and the imperfections that have held us back from living in this type of love.

I used to think I had to make myself worthy of it, that it was something I could *do*, something to earn. And so I went about trying to earn it. I clutched my rosary with gusto and recited my prayers with a holy vigor in a desperate attempt to be accepted by Him. But now I see the fallacy in that.

Christ gives His love freely. He gives His love to the broken, to the cheater, to the thief, to the addict. He gives His love to me and to you, dear sister. He has made us worthy.

Can you accept that?

I know the lies that can swirl around in your mind. And sometimes those lies we have been taught to believe about ourselves are the root of why we don't allow God to truly father us, why we don't fully accept His love. We hold out the filters of our fallen fathers and place them up to Him, somehow believing that He too will fall short in providing.

The truth is that we all have something impeding our trust in God as Father—some lies that we have come to believe about ourselves, or some lies we have come to believe about Him. Maybe you feel unlovable, unseen, undervalued. Maybe you question His love, His mercy, His providence.

Whatever it is, hope remains for you.

"We are God's children now," Saint John reminds us (v. 2). Sister, you have been adopted into His family, into His perfect and unrelenting love. You, with your weary heart and your doubtful mind, have a place here.

So go to Him as a child would—unguarded and unafraid, expectant of His love and providence in your life. And if you happen to find yourself surrounded by the shadows of your past, run to the Light. He is waiting to bring you home.

READING: 1 JOHN 3:1–2

- Regardless of the hardships of your childhood and struggles experienced by your family, you are sought after by God the Father. If it's been a while, turn to Him and pray an "Our Father" from a place of childlike trust.
- Do you mother someone in your life? As a close confidant or spiritual mother? Take time to remind them of the spiritual reality that God is their heavenly Father who will never leave.

You belong to Christ.

1 Corinithians 3:23

WEEK 13
THE BATTLE FOR
MY BODY
Young Adulthood

T he question came to me on a hot day in the middle of the summer. I only really know this, I suppose, because of the sticky popsicle juice that had dropped straight into my bare lap. That's when I noticed them—my thighs. As my mother and I sat side by side in our bathing suits on the patio swing, I looked down and began to pay attention to the particular way my legs took up space, the way they flattened against the wood beneath them.

"Why do my legs touch when I sit?" I asked my mother with the childlike ignorance of an eleven-year-old. "It's normal," I remember her saying. "Everyone's legs do that."

But whatever she told me that day wasn't enough. From that moment on, I began to dig for the answers myself. And I found them, eventually, in the magazines that lined my bedside table and the music videos I used to sneak in while my mom was asleep. *No, your legs were not supposed to touch*, I decided, and that was the seed that grew into my battle with body image.

By the time I was twenty-one, I weighed ninety-eight pounds. I had come to the conclusion by then that eating was not worth it, that the prize of "the right size" meant more than that ham and cheese sandwich everyone was always trying to get me to eat. "I'm worried about you," they'd say as they tossed a bag of chips into my hands. But it didn't matter what anyone said. I wasn't looking for their approval. The only approval I needed came from the scale and the reflection I saw in the mirror each day.

It took years for me to recognize the damage I was doing to my body, years to shed the lies about the way a woman should look. And even now, the lies still creep in. I catch them in the mirror when I see the cellulite on the back of my legs or in the pictures that require me to confront the way my hips jut out.

You're fat is usually how it starts. It's the first whisper my brain recites until I am able to halt the deeply rooted damage my mind was trained to inflict. It is a recurring thought waging war on my confidence, one that seeks to undermine the beauty God has planted in the curves and the hips He has uniquely given me. But I know now that these thoughts deceive, that there is a greater truth about me, and that it is a truth worth fighting for.

In today's scripture passage, we read, "For the wisdom of this world is foolishness with God" (1 Corinthians 3:19). I wonder what sort of "wisdom" might you be listening to?

The world is quick to teach us. It's quick to find those vulnerable bits of ourselves and undermine God's truth spoken into us. Maybe the whispers you've been hearing have made you believe that you're ugly or weak or unlovable. Maybe they have even grown so loud that you have begun to hate yourself.

I don't know your particular story, or the mistakes you've made up to this point, or whether you have allowed the wisdom of the world to color the view of who you are. I don't know if you drown out the pain through your liquor cabinet or self-harm or people-pleasing.

Regardless, a love story is written right on the pages of your Bible. It is a story that is waiting to drown out the whispers that cripple your tired mind, a story that can renew and restore and forgive if only you let it.

So, as you ponder today's scripture, let His love wash over your fear and release you from the restraints that have held you captive for so long. Let it fill you with His truth and inspire you with His grace.

You are uniquely and wonderfully made, and a seat made just for you waits right here at His table. "You belong to Christ," Saint Paul tells us (v. 23). And that truth can silence those whispers the world has been feeding you, if you let it.

Pull up your chair, sister. Let us feast on His love.

READING: 1 CORINTHIANS 3:19–23

- How is your relationship with your body? If you struggle with discontentment over lines, aging, curves, or not being what you perceive as "fitting the ideal," take a deep breath. Christ includes you in those who belong to Him, and He has no measuring tape.
- Whose voice are you listening to? Tune in to Christ's voice today: you belong to Him.

We live to the Lord.

Romans 14:8

WEEK 14
CROSSING THE LINE
AND CROSSING BACK
Rite of Passage

The place smelled of alcohol and musty carpet. It was my first time in a bar, and by American standards, I was too young to be there. But the loophole for my presence that night was a Canadian one because we had just crossed the border.

I didn't know then that crossing over into that uncharted territory also meant crossing over into uncharted experiences. It was my first time on foreign soil, my first time trying alcohol, and my first time watching someone snort cocaine off a dirty table.

I could sense my heart's discord as I watched that thin, white line disappear into his nose, but what did I expect? It was the music industry, and I was touring with a rock band that sang love songs dedicated to narcotics.

And so I did what any flighty nineteen-year-old would do. I shoved the discomfort down with a couple of tortilla chips and hearty swigs of vodka. I had decided to go on that tour because I thought it would be good to add to my résumé, and it did set me up for "success." I came home to a new job title and an official spot on the record label's payroll, a step above my internship status.

The job provided even more "experience" than I bargained for.

Soon, the culture of the industry surrounded me, and I found myself in situations that made that night in Canada seem mild—an appetizer to the main course I hadn't ordered in the first place.

All the while, every Sunday my back would rub up against a wooden pew as my fingers would thumb their way through a tattered Roman Missal. It was my reprieve, my break for fresh air in the middle of the pollution that filled my soul during the week.

I felt the chasm in me grow the widest whenever I sat in those pews. It was a weekly reminder of just how far off my compass had gone. I was a walking contradiction with a Bible in one hand and a drink in the other. Still, I tried everything to force those two worlds together. I wanted to ride the line between living with acceptance from the world while keeping my faith intact, but the gap between them grew until I had no choice but to jump.

Two years after that night in Canada, I finally made the leap. I could feel the nerves course through my body as I marched over to Human Resources, resignation letter in hand. "You're crazy," they told me because they knew how hard I had worked to get there.

I had passed their guidelines for belonging and finally was one of them. And the thing about it is I *was* crazy, but only because I had been living contrary to how I was being called to live.

Today's reading to meditate on from Saint Paul reminds us, "We do not live to ourselves, and we do not die to ourselves. If we live, we live to the Lord, and if we die, we die to the Lord" (Romans 14:7–8).

Sister, the world will teach you a million different ways to find your belonging, rites of passage required for acceptance. Maybe you feel the pressure to belong coming from your sorority or your boyfriend or your job, and so you surrender with the alcohol or the sex or the parties. But surrendering leaves a rift in our hearts because our belonging isn't found anywhere other than Him. It is in Him and for Him and through Him that we are meant to live. Trying to do it any other way will just leave us empty.

I know you're looking for your place in this world. I know you can feel lonely and unlovable and downright worthless a lot of the time. It's easy to find validation by living for ourselves—by trying the drug or telling the lie. But our belonging isn't tied to anything we do or don't do. Our belonging is tied to who we are.

Sister, you are a daughter of God, and He is calling you.

READING: ROMANS 14:7-9

- Do you feel like you're living the life you were called to live or coming up short against your own expectations? Quiet your mind and take time for prayer to discern this question: who am I living for?
- In what ways is Jesus calling you to "die" in your life? What is keeping you back from living more authentically? Be honest with yourself and be gentle.

◇

Continue in what you have learned and firmly believed. 2 Timothy 3:14

THE SURPRISE SEEDLING
OF A FRIENDSHIP

School

The darkened spots on her skin were unmistakable. They were the reason she hurt, the reason she hid, and the reason the kids all snickered behind her back. No one knew what they were or what caused them, and no one cared to know until her mother ended up in front of our eighth-grade class right before our big field trip to the beach.

Her voice cracked as she explained her daughter's condition. She told us about the tumors that crushed her nerves and the resulting pain. But mostly, she told us about the tears of fear. For weeks leading up to this trip, her daughter worried about what the other kids would think of her exposed skin in a bathing suit.

Something broke open in me that day because as I sat and listened to her mother's plea for kindness, I felt a nudge—a little invitation to an unsought friendship.

I accepted, though it did not come without consequences. I knew I'd be forced to leave the safety of the approval I had garnered from my peers. I knew I'd have to forge my own path.

The waves of judgment about our friendship rolled in one after the other in varying degrees of force. They washed away my friendships, social status, and overall sense of belonging in the world. But looking back now, I see the gifts that sprang forth from the turmoil.

I couldn't have anticipated the plan that God would unfurl through our friendship, that she would eventually be my maid of honor, and that I would eventually be hers. I couldn't have seen the concerts we'd scream our way through or the late nights we'd stay up talking or the tears we'd both cry on the day her father died. I just knew, sitting there in my eighth-grade class, that God had planted a seed and I was responsible for its growth.

It wasn't always easy to get it to sprout because I was still pouring it out into friendships that were phony as I sought a frivolous social status. That little seed didn't fully flourish until I stopped trying to find my place of belonging in others, until I let God's word direct my actions.

I'm not always good at listening to God's promptings. More often than not, His words get lost in the chaos of my days. But the gospel speaks loudly if you let it lead you to follow the nudges He places in your heart. You may lose friends and status. But so much beauty awaits.

Our scripture for today reminds us that "everyone who belongs to God may be proficient, equipped for every good work" (2 Timothy 3:17).

The realization that you belong to Christ comes with a responsibility, one rooted in trust, in knowing your place in His wonderful plan and allowing it to dictate your response. It is a cooperation with grace. You, dear sister, are "equipped for every good work," as we hear in today's reading. You are strong and capable and ready.

And I know you may fear what He is asking of you. I know you may feel His gentle nudge on your heart and worry late into the night about the job you might lose or the friends that might leave if you follow it. The waves look scary; it's true. They look big and powerful and intimidating. But, sister, you have been given a great responsibility. You have been called to swim.

Something marvelous waits for you in those waves, something He is waiting to teach you, or some way He is waiting to reach you. Dive in, sister. Leave your fear and your stress on the shore. Allow Him to carry you to safety.

And when the waves threaten to swallow you whole, when you're kicking and screaming for help, look to Him. He will be your lifeline.

And just keep swimming.

READING: 2 TIMOTHY 3:14–17

- Do you look back on a person from school who stood out and feel proud of how you treated them? If not, examine how that lesson may be repeating itself in life now. Either way, offer a prayer for that person.
- When God is gently calling you, how do you experience His voice? In silent prayer, at Mass or Adoration, through song and vocal prayer? Listen with extra attention.

$$\diamond$$

We are children of God. Romans 8:26

WEEK 16

SEEKING FAMILY,
FINDING GOD

Family of Origin

H i, I'm your uncle," he said, as I slid my hand into his. He was a stranger to me, someone I could have passed unknowingly on the street. They were all strangers in that room, all unfamiliar faces living unfamiliar lives.

I hadn't planned for it to be this way. But I suppose no one picks their father's funeral as the location to meet their family for the first time. Yet, there I was, shaking hands with a stranger whose same bloodline coursed through my veins.

Still, I scanned for any hint that would tie me to them. And the harder I looked, the more I saw it. The same thin-lipped smiles and wide-knuckled fingers I was used to seeing in my own reflection were sprinkled throughout the room.

And I desperately wanted to be loved by them, to be known and welcomed. "I hope they like me," I had said to my husband as I walked out the door that day. But my desire to belong wasn't realistic, at least not in the way I wanted it to be, because they had spent whole lifetimes together.

Birthdays, setbacks, celebrations—they all carried the same experiences. Time knit them together in a way that I couldn't quickly be woven in. I was the real stranger there in the room that day, an onlooker to the family with whom I shared nothing beyond a last name.

I never did talk to my family again after the day of the funeral. But I tried, I did. I sent messages and condolences and offered hope to their hurting hearts. Silence was their only response. And it was the silence that deafened the truth in my heart. I couldn't ignore the lies that silence screamed into my soul.

You are not loved, it said. And I believed it.

I let the lies fester and turn into the chains that held me back from truly experiencing the freedom found in God's love. My belief in His love for me was tied up in belonging to a group of people. I should have been seeking only Him. Instead, I put the expectation of His love into the hands of individuals unwilling to deliver it.

I'm sure this is familiar to you. We've all carried the deep desire of belonging over to a group or a person or a family member who has denied it. We so often seek out our place among imperfect individuals and then expect perfect acceptance in return. And in this mismanaged expectation we allow lies to speak into who we are, lies that prevent us from fully living in God's love.

And I think we experience it more often than we realize. It can sneak into even the most ordinary moments of our days. When the darkness is illuminated by the harsh glow of our phones each night, we are bombarded with all of the friends who went to all of the gatherings we weren't invited to.

And I wonder, dear sister, what is the lie you tell yourself when you sit alone in the night? Do you feel worthless? Alone? Unlovable?

In today's reading, Saint Paul wrote, "For you did not receive a spirit of slavery to fall back into fear, but you have received a spirit of adoption" (Romans 8:15).

A sort of slavery happens when we look to others to fill what only God can fill. It is a slavery full of the lies we've been told about ourselves, be it from a friend, mentor, or parent. It can hold your mind captive, making you believe you are someone other than who God says you are. And so we often bounce from person to person to find our worth, always searching for our place of belonging in the world, and always being let down by it.

But you have been adopted, dear sister. A perfect Father with a perfect love waits to welcome you, to speak freedom and life into your tired heart. Go to Him. When the weight of the world's rejection shackles you with lies about who you are, truth is waiting.

And it will set you free.

READING: ROMANS 8:14–17

- If you feel like an outsider in your family because you are simply not close or you have been shut out, how can you turn that desire to belong back to your relationship with the Lord?
- Our (imperfect) families will let us down, but they can also lift us up. Think about a time you've been supported by a family member. Pray for that person now.

Keep up your courage. Acts 27:25

WEEK 17

FREEDOM FROM SOCIAL BOXING

Friendship

The neighborhood kids were zipping around us on their bikes as I felt the anxiety surge in my throat. And I suddenly wished I could be one of them again, pedaling faster and faster away from the conflicting ideas that adults were passing back and forth.

It was hot that evening, and the summer sun was fading behind us. We stood outside on the concrete driveway that had been baking in the heat all day. Politics and religion were the points of conversation that night. I suppose the memo from their grandparents about such topics being advised against never did trickle down to them. And so, in between our watchful warnings about incoming cars and our quick interludes to kiss any skinned knees, we discussed and debated.

The most accurate way to describe it would be to say that *they* discussed and debated the issues at hand. They argued over the right to choose and shared their opinions on faith in America. And it was mostly amicable, sure. We were grown adult friends who could handle the hard stuff.

Still, I felt a line between the group wedge right down the middle of the opposing arguments. And that's where I stood, on that thin, safe line, offering small nods or smiles to those whom I felt needed it—a "get back in there" sort of nudge, an Adrian to the Rockys in the ring.

I can be a great cheerleader. If you decide you ever want to get out in that ring and fight the good fight, I'll be your water girl. And even if the issues you are fighting for go against everything I believe to be true, I'll find some sort of commonality and rally behind it.

But I'm a terrible fighter despite having my own beliefs. They are beliefs rooted in the truth of the teachings of the Catholic Church, yet all it takes is one quick sucker punch in that arena, and I falter. My heart begins to pound; my hands begin to shake; my legs begin to buckle. And so, while the brawl takes place on that small, square mat, I watch while others do the dirty work.

This has always been true for me. Revealing my true self for others to judge has always felt too risky. The simple act of speaking out about a topic someone else disagrees with often sends a shock wave of anxiety straight through me. I conceal myself and walk that thin, safe line.

It's not something I'm exactly proud of, but it's something I grew up learning to do. Staying silent was a way for me to keep the peace while bipolar flare-ups often ripped through my family. I didn't want to be a target of someone else's anger, so I learned to fade into the safety of silence.

Maybe you also stand with your back against the ropes to feel safe instead of getting in that ring. You can't be judged there. You are free from the spectators' watchful glares.

But at times you are meant to go out into the ring, to stand alone in that spotlight. Sister, do not let the fear of rejection keep you from being authentic to yourself. Do not let it stop you from getting out there and proclaiming what He has asked you to proclaim. "I urge you now to keep up the courage," today's scripture for reflection reminds us (Acts 27:22).

I know how badly you want to belong, to feel the love that comes from being accepted. And I know you fear what He is whispering into your heart, that you shrink in the face of the world's rejection. I know because I feel it too. But something deeper inside of you wants to break free, doesn't it? Something calls you forward, inching you into that spotlight.

The courage you are looking for is not in the security of the darkness you would like to sink into. It is not in the silence or the safety of the middle. The courage you are looking for is found in the Holy Spirit who gives you His strength.

Come out of hiding, dear sister. God has granted you safety.

READING: ACTS 27:22–24

- If you find it challenging to be true to yourself, what small habit can you shift to be more authentic, whether that is to simply to speak less or avoid prolonged conversations where you feel tempted to hide?
- Consider a time someone has listened respectfully in friendship to your views and consider what you have learned from that encounter. Is there room for listening in friendship?

◇

"Let no one separate." Matthew 19:6

WEEK 18

THE UNKNOWNS OF OUR FERTILITY JOURNEY

Romantic Relationship

I steadied myself over the onion as I sliced into its crisp core. It was a rookie mistake because one should *never* lean over an onion. Alas, the tears began to flow as the knife released the invasive scent into our newly leased apartment kitchen.

"Why didn't you warn me about this?" I later asked my mother through the telephone wires I relied on to close the gap on our new-found distance. A freshly married woman should be prepared for certain things, and this seemed important enough to be one of them.

I learned a lot in those first few years of marriage, by asking my mother and making mistakes. Nearly a decade later, I found myself on the opposite end of the country with wet cheeks for a different reason.

"Why didn't anybody warn us about this?" I sobbed into my husband's shoulder. We never found any good answers for our infertility, not even from our doctors after years of treatment.

Looking back now, I can see why it was so difficult for me to let go of finding those answers. When life got tricky, I'd often find myself running back to safety for the answers, back to my place of belonging. In those early years of marriage, it was my mother's wisdom I found my refuge in. But after a few years of lessons on burnt bread and conflict resolution, I soon found a new source of answers: my husband.

The beautiful thing about marriage is that it allows you to be vulnerable. Security resides in our marriage vows. "In sickness and health, for better or worse"—it is in these promises that we often find our freedom. It is why our spouse usually bears the brunt of our fiery rage, or why they have the unusual advantage of seeing us in a stained pair of sweats from yesterday morning's breakfast. The more you know you belong, the freer you are to be authentic.

But these wonderful marital promises can also become a hiding place. This was true for me. Infertility was always that big question mark in our lives, the one thing no one could give me the answers to—not even my husband. Even so, I looked to him to find them.

The truth is that these answers can really only ever come from God—our ultimate place of belonging. And I didn't truly believe I belonged to Him. I'd pray, sure—beg even! But I never felt as though I could be vulnerable enough to fully let go and trust Him with this issue.

Today's reading for reflection tells us, "For this reason a man shall leave his father and mother and be joined to his wife, and the two shall become one flesh" (Matthew 19:5).

Through the union of marriage, we are made one and have been given a place of belonging in Him. We are called to cling to each other while also seeking Him together. It becomes easy to run to your safe spot for the answers to those big and painful questions in your life without also bringing them to Christ. It's easy to find safety and comfort in the security of the marriage covenant alone, or in any other place you find your belonging.

But, sister, let go. Loosen the grip of control just a little bit. A place for you to find your rest exists. Listen, I know you may be tired. I know the answers may not come and your heart can grow weary. I know sometimes prayers feel weak and trust begins to wane.

Bring it to Him. Bring your broken heart and your tired soul and your doubtful mind. Come as you are. Right in the middle of that heartache, love is waiting to welcome you in. It is a love that offers freedom. You can come broken and still be accepted. You can come vulnerable and still be loved. You can come downright angry and still belong.

The answers you are looking for are found in Him.

READING: MATTHEW 19:4–6

- Think about a marriage in your life that has taught you about trust. Celebrate the example with a prayer of gratitude.
- Do you struggle with wanting to know what is to come in your relationships? Take this to the Lord, trust that you already belong to Him, and ask Him to foster grace in your relationships.

We have received grace.

Romans 1:5

WEEK 19

CHOOSING DIGNITY
OVER THE JOB

Workplace

T hey really want this to be sexy," I remember her saying. The request came as a mumble through the speaker on my phone. Being a dancer isn't always just about the art form; it's also about the look. It's about the skirts that rise just a little higher or the shirts that hang just a little lower.

In this case, it was about the lingerie. "Whatever shows the most skin," said her voicemail.

The people pleaser in me began to balk in fear as her words collided with my conscience. The people pleaser in me doesn't like to utter the word *no*. The people pleaser in me prefers to nod to whatever is requested.

I didn't know if I was allowed to disagree, or if doing so would cost me the job I had already been hired to do. I just knew that dancing in lingerie in front of a few hundred sets of eyes went against some very personal and tightly held beliefs. I knew that not saying something was actually saying everything, that it defied what I believed in as a Christian.

I waited for the right words before calling her back. I wanted to say something, anything, that would make me sound less prudish, to let her know that I was still a team player despite my reluctance.

The words never came. As I held the phone to my ear, all I could think to squeak out was, "Uh, I don't really wear that sort of thing."

A certain sort of adaptability is expected of dancers. You'll be asked to accommodate the varying visions of the projects you are hired to do. And it's easy to get lost in it, to lose yourself in the make-it-or-break-it world of endless competition. Someone is always next in line waiting to take your place, ready to do what you won't.

When I picked up the phone to express my discomfort, I knew the possibility loomed of losing my job to the next person. But I also knew I had a higher obligation and my place of belonging didn't hinge on my willingness to conform. My place of belonging was already fixed in God, and that was where my accountability resided.

The phone call that day was difficult for me to follow through with. It was uncomfortable and scary. But it was also freeing because somewhere buried deep in my *no* was a tiny whisper of a *yes*. It was a *yes* to Him, a *yes* to me, and a *yes* to living in a way that I was proud of.

That tiny *yes* carried me all the way to that stage, fully clothed and with my dignity still intact. That tiny *yes* saved me.

Saint Paul reminds us in today's reading that we are "called to be saints." We are "called to belong to Jesus Christ" (Romans 1:6–7).

The world will fight back. It will pressure you into compliance and entice you with acceptance. It will plead and scream for your allegiance. But your life is meant to look different, dear sister. It is meant to be lived with His call on your heart and those tiny *yeses* on your lips. It is meant to "bring about the obedience of faith among all the Gentiles for the sake of his name" (v. 5).

And I know this sort of responsibility is hard because swimming upstream is exhausting. It's cumbersome and downright embarrassing a lot of the time, but He will provide the grace necessary for the journey. Liberation awaits in your *yes* because when you find your belonging in Him, the world no longer has a stake in your approval. It no longer dictates your response.

Sister, I don't know what demands the world is currently whispering into your ear. I don't know where the pressure to belong is coming from or if the people pleaser in you shrinks with fear like the people pleaser in me does. But you were made for more. You were made for freedom and love and belonging. You were made for Him.

An abundance of *yeses* waits to be found in your *no*. So, when the world's whispers fill your head with the pressure to fit in, keep your eyes tilted upward with your heart set on Him, and just say *no*.

READING: ROMANS 1:4–7

- Have you been asked to do something that felt like crossing the line at work? Ask Jesus to go through the memory with you and feel His presence.
- Where in your life can you say *no* right now that will actually open you up for more *yeses*? Ask the Holy Spirit to help you in saying *yes*.

You were washed. 1 Corinthians 6:11

WEEK 20

AN ARMY OF SUPPORT

Church Community

I used to hate the interrogation at dinner parties. The typical "What's your name? What do you do? Are you married?" always felt a little intrusive. But I had my one-liners to quell the curiosity of the strangers on the other end of my handshake. "My name is Brittany. I work in Public Relations. I've been married for eight years."

It hardly ever stopped there. "Any kids?" they'd often ask with curiosity dripping from their tongues. I always knew I could expect the question after years of marriage. Still, no matter how practiced I was at it, the answer was never quite clear. "No . . ." I'd say, feeling like I needed to clarify. A big asterisk came with that answer, a need to explain away the shame that came with our infertility. I became an expert at bottling up my reality into a neat and perfect package. "No, I don't have kids, but my husband and I are enjoying each other right now."

Infertility always felt so isolating, like something about it was unconscionable to speak about publicly. And I have never been one to dish out my problems into someone else's bowl. We all have our things we like to keep private.

I wanted everyone to think I had it together, that I didn't go home and cry each time someone asked me that depressing question. And for a while, I had them all fooled. I let the pressure from the pain build inside, careful to keep the secret close.

I carried that shame around with me until I couldn't carry it anymore, couldn't hide it away in my silent tears at night or shove it down with a fake smile and some nice pleasantries. Eight years into our struggle, the words began to flow, my heart began to open, and the ache began to empty. I finally shared the reason for our quiet home.

I poured it out onto the shoulders of so many, and together they lifted that heavy load with their generous prayers, heartfelt notes, and helpful advice. Suddenly, I wasn't alone in the fight, and my answer to that daunting dinner party question didn't seem quite so intimidating because now a whole army of people I couldn't have known before was ready to wage this war with me.

I still remember my shock at the empathy and the compassion and the commiserating words from some when I finally let it out. "Me too," they'd often say, and for the first time in a long time, I didn't feel so alone. I was a part of a family, a community of people who were with me to fight and to rally and to encourage me through the heartache.

We are made for community. Today's reading to ponder reminds us we all belong to the Mystical Body of Christ: "But you were washed, you were sanctified, you were justified in the name of the Lord Jesus Christ and in the Spirit of our God" (1 Corinthians 6:11). To this end, Saint Paul points us to our baptism. We have all been washed and sanctified and justified through this sacrament. And, likewise, we have all been counted, because through baptism we are not only saved from our sins, but we are also brought into a family. We don't strive to live a life of virtue alone; we are called to do it in and through community.

Sister, I don't know what load you are carrying right now, or whether your arms are beginning to buckle under the weight of it.

But an army is waiting for you too. This army will pray with you and fight for you and carry you through the thick of it.

I know it's hard to let go. I know it can make you feel weak and burdensome and shameful at times, but you were not meant to struggle alone. Open hearts and eager arms wait to help lift the weight you are holding on to.

So, the next time your tears begin to fall heavy from the burden of a hidden pain, let it go. We are holding you, sister. You are not alone anymore.

READING: 1 CORINTHIANS 6:11

- Is there something in your story that has kept you feeling separate from your church community? Seek out the safe and listening ears of others because they will hold the space for your wounds.
- Think about the women you know through your church community. Who could use extra love and prayers? Reach out to someone this week to let her know she is seen and loved.

✧

"They have believed that you sent me." John 17:8

WEEK 21

SOAK IN THE STARS

Relationship with the Lord

I could feel the tiny pinch of a hundred different mosquitoes colliding with my legs that night. *You'll regret this tomorrow*, I thought, but the magnificent North Georgia sky called my attention upward. Something was magical about the way the thick summer air enveloped me that evening, and the way the stars seemed to plead for my attention. I relished it. With my head craned back against the stiff, wooden chair, I marveled at the constellations, wondered at the galaxies, and felt God invite me into something higher.

Still, I could feel the pull of the earth calling me back down to it. Emails needed to be answered and meals needed to be prepared. With my son sleeping soundly in the room behind me, I knew this rare minute alone was an opportunity for me to be more productive, to "capture the moment."

A war began to rage within me. Right underneath that expansive sky, the gentle call to the heavens clashed with the big, boisterous work screaming for my attention down below.

More often than not, my legs are rearing to run and my hands are eager to work. I dive straight into every unchecked task on my to-do list and race until bedtime greets me at the end of each day.

But that night was different. That night I stopped. I let the beauty of His creation beguile my heart and call me upward to Him.

Sometimes the most productive thing you can do is to sit back and let God woo you—to look around, to take it in, to just . . . be.

I've never been good at that. In fact, I am an expert at doing just the opposite. The light and buzz and ding of my phone are in constant competition with the piles and stacks and demands of my house. Another text always needs answering or a dish needs washing. Life is busy, and so I've learned to run, run, run—always doing, doing, doing—in a frantic attempt to cross an imaginary finish line.

And I've noticed that this frenzied approach to life often carries over into my relationship with Christ. I'm quick to "do" whatever is required of me; I recite the rosary; I go to Mass. But I'm terrible at stopping long enough to allow God's love and beauty to penetrate my heart.

And this constant state of action, it feels awfully productive. We experience the allure of checking things off lengthy to-do lists and speeding through to the next thing, and then the next. But like any relationship, we need a balance between giving and receiving. And sometimes, it is in the pause that our hearts finally grow silent enough to accept what God has given us. It is in the pause that we find life.

I'm sure this is familiar to you because our culture prides itself on outward productivity. The more things you can juggle between your two insufficient hands, the better. And so you race. You wake up tired from the marathon of yesterday only to compete in it again today.

In today's reading, Saint John shared Jesus speaking to God the Father, "Now they know that everything you have given me is from you" (John 17:7). God gives so that you may receive. And I wonder, dear sister, what might you be missing while your hands are busy juggling the frenzy of life? School schedules, birthday parties, playdates—it's all so heavy to hold, isn't it? But while your head is buried in your phone as you try to climb out of the mounting assortment of notifications, respite awaits just beyond it. Radiant sunsets and grassy fields and expansive mountain ranges all beckon for your attention.

Look up. God is waiting to speak through His creation; He is waiting to woo you with wonder for the gifts He has laid out before you.

And I hope you receive them. Everything we are given comes from Him. It is all a gift meant to call us upward, to breathe life into our weary hearts. We need only stop long enough to accept it.

You don't have to try so hard, dear sister. The race has already been won.

READING: JOHN 17:6–8

- How crowded does your life feel? Give yourself permission to clear out some space, to say *no*, and to remember how seen and known you are by God.
- Take a moment for gratitude. Count your blessings, starting with the little things and adding up to the big ones. Notice how particularly you are loved and belong to God's family.

PART 3

BELOVED

by Leana Bowler

Set aside the myth that your lovability as a woman relies on how you are treated by other people, what your life circumstances have been, or how your story has unfolded to this point. Instead, accept this invitation from the Lord to fully embrace your identity and worth as being made in His image and likeness. You are infinitely and unconditionally loved by God.

We walk through ten stories from my life, ten unique stages from early childhood through adolescence to mature adulthood, which are paired with illuminating scripture passages. We encourage you to open your Bible and follow along. Take time with the questions and let them sit inside your heart.

Clothe yourselves with love.

Colossians 3:14

WEEK 22
LONGING FOR NORMALCY
Childhood

I sat cross-legged on the living room floor captivated by the streaks of sunlight like rainbows at my grandparents' house. My hands were raised, attempting to catch them, when my mom walked in with the letter from my stepdad.

His handwriting was barely legible. Dark marks smudged across the wrinkled notebook paper. I imagined him sitting on the edge of his cot, lips moving as he sounded out each word, stumbling over spelling, and erasing over and over.

He had committed armed robbery and was arrested on the same day I lost my two front teeth. I placed each tooth under my pillow and listened as the adults in the other room discussed what he had done and how many years he would serve behind bars.

I hugged my tattered Cabbage Patch doll and thought of the time I watched him get into a fistfight with his friend in a parking lot, knocking out his friend's tooth. I wondered if the tooth fairy had given his friend a pair of shiny quarters. Initial shock gave way to quiet resentment when I saw his mug shot on the evening news and realized other people saw it too.

Later that year, we moved to my grandparents' home permanently.

My stepdad's letters kept coming. I worried endlessly that my identity was now rooted in something bad, unable to receive love, seemingly unforgivable. Glaring imperfections stood amid the squeaky-clean image of our new suburban life. I wanted a normal dad like everyone around us: a dad who went to work, loved baseball, and was not in prison.

I questioned whether these desires made me a bad daughter. I had to learn that comparison would not bring healing but would instead push me further into the void of shame. And Jesus did not want me there. I was loved by Him, and my family was rooted in His goodness.

Even though my family was messy and broken, I wanted everyone to know we loved, laughed, played, fought, and made amends. The suffering we shared and worked through refined me, instructed me in the ways of mercy, and taught me how to love others with compassion. The work of healing meant toiling away at the most tender scars on my heart by asking the Lord for His reminder that I was seen and loved.

Maybe you hold the hurtful moments of your childhood in this way: enduring the tension of caring for people who are imperfect, struggling not to view them through the lens of their most "unlovable" moments, contending with the lies that Christ sees you through the lens of your own so-called "unlovable" moments.

Let us contemplate today's scripture verse: "As God's chosen ones, holy and beloved, clothe yourselves with compassion, kindness, humility, meekness, and patience" (Colossians 3:12). And as we pray, let our hearts focus on how we are chosen, holy, and beloved by God. Allow the love of God to fill you with peace. Set before Him your family and invite Him to pour out healing over the areas where their brokenness has hurt you and made you feel ashamed.

Sister, Christ alone has the authority to tell you who you are, and He says you are loved. Maybe you feel the burden of the sins of your past, broken relationships, or times when you were overwhelmed and reacted in a way you deeply regret. As you reflect on being holy and beloved, I invite you to listen with your heart to the gentle voice of Our Lord who calls you *forgiven and beloved*.

No, we are not defined by our most broken moments. We are capable of forgiving and being forgiven, loving and being loved. We are rooted in our real identity as beloved daughters, never too wounded for the Savior of the world. He pours forgiveness from His own wounds to cover yours. God's mercy cover every inch of your entire being held close to His heart and endlessly loved.

READING: COLOSSIANS 3:12–14

- Have you felt defined by your most broken moments? Take this pain to Our Lord for comfort in prayer.
- Is there someone in your life you judged or gossiped about because of what you learned about her family member or someone close to her? Take that to the person and take it to Jesus in the sacrament of confession.

I will know fully. 1 Corinthians 13:12

WEEK 23

FALSE PERFECTION

Young Adulthood

The night air was cold and damp, blanketing my bare skin as I hurried out the door to my friends' car with music blaring in our quiet neighborhood, leaving a trail of dried fallen leaves as the tires screeched. I pulled down the visor, as usual, checking my face to ensure that I looked perfect and rolling my eyes in annoyance before slamming the visor shut.

When we arrived at the party, a feeling of apprehension passed over my heart. I felt a sudden longing to go back home and laugh alongside my family with a face scrubbed clean.

But my trepidations quickly vanished as my friend and I linked arms and headed inside. The guy I was seeing was there, making his usual crude remarks at my expense. I laughed along with everyone else. He was using me, and I was using him. It was mutual disregard for each other hidden by a false idea of love.

The night ended like most nights. I crept inside my house and flinched at the loud click as I locked the door. I caught a glimpse of my face in the dining room mirror. Thick makeup smudged in the corners of my eyes that looked vacant, sad, tired.

On the corner shelf was a statue of Our Lady. She looked beautiful. I looked back in the mirror and heard her motherly voice in my heart, *Those people are not your friends.*

I was a prisoner to a shallow sense of perfection based exclusively on my appearance, on how I would be seen on the surface, but nothing beyond that. My confidence was low. Skin too flawed. Nose too big. Lips too small—all imaginary defects that I believed were real, defects that I believed would determine who I was and would become. I refused to acknowledge more beneath the exterior.

Inside, I longed for God and for His love. I desired to know Jesus, but I was afraid of what loving Him would require. All the walls would have to crumble, and I would be revealed. The broken parts of me would need to be mended. Healing was work, and I did not want to do it.

Instead, I went with the crowd. I allowed the influence of my friends to pull me along, like a fragile leaf carried by the wind with no destination. Everything was *fine*. I went willingly, brushing aside the humiliation when I felt I had gone too far.

However, when I was confronted with the truth that night, I decided to take all of the dark sins on my heart to the sacrament of confession. I rested beneath His downpour of mercy and rejoiced as the grime of sin was washed away. He soothed the pain that afflicted me and strengthened my soul. This is where His love led me: to a place of fullness and faith.

Sister, today's scripture for reflection tells us, "For now we see in a mirror, dimly, but then we will see face to face" (1 Corinthians 13:11). Maybe you have gone through a time when your vision was clouded, a period in your life when your sin felt heavy, your life felt void of purpose, and you could not see a way forward.

You might find yourself currently in a period of shame and uncertainty. The truth in today's verse is your way forward. Jesus awaits you on this path, and His mercy calls out to you. Christ's love for you, a love that is not superficial but sacrificial, calls your name.

You can turn away from the people and the things that only seek to exploit your inherent dignity. Or you can encourage a daughter, a sister, or a friend to seek the heart of Jesus as she struggles with her own sense of God's love for her.

Jesus sees us unveiled, stripped of the veneers we often operate behind. He sees the deepest parts of our being, and He enters into the places that we feel are too ugly and too dark. That is what Christ does with our brokenness. He transforms it with His redemptive love and there, in that place of open surrender, illuminated in splendor, we see His glory.

READING: 1 CORINTHIANS 13:11–13

- Has your belovedness hinged on romantic pursuits or friendships that weren't healthy for you? Remind yourself who loves you unconditionally: He who loved you first.
- Is there an opportunity in your life to reach out to a woman struggling with her lovability? Maybe even for you to share vulnerably about your own struggle in this area?

✧

In all these things we are more.

Romans 8:37

HER BIRTH BREAKING
AND HEALING US

Rite of Passage

T he sound of her heartbeat was a soft *whoosh* that soothed my restlessness as I confronted the unfamiliar sensations of labor. I listened and leaned forward, my grip increasing on the railing of the hospital bed. Deep breaths. The faint smell of antiseptic blended with the remnants of my perfume.

Outside the hospital room, fireworks glittered across the ebony sky. It was New Year's Eve. I was twenty years old and about to give birth to my daughter. This child held within my body would soon blink her little eyes against the brightness of this world. My young body had transformed, softened, and expanded in order to give this precious new soul life.

"Here she comes!"

A palpable elation flooded the room as her impressive cry rang out. The warmth of her silky skin pressed against mine, unleashing joyful tears. My body now displayed the ripples and wrinkles of her exist-ence. I marveled as she moved her tiny head and opened her mouth in search of food. I instinctively pressed her cheek against my chest until she found it. I watched my husband blink back tears, his baseball cap covering his honey brown hair that matched hers.

Our daughter, beauty born from brokenness. This little girl revealed to me the power of God's love from the first moment she flailed her tiny limbs and took her first breath. Years of trauma and sexual sin had obscured God's love for me. My flesh had felt defiled, shallow, and void of grace, far from the presence of God because of how I had seen my body as a commodity, a shell to be put on display for the pleasure of others. A form with no other purpose than to be consumed and then discarded. Flaws to be critiqued and artificially concealed. False perfection was necessary to determine its worth, a glossy false finish.

Then motherhood dissolved these inaccurate notions. I felt the closeness of God's hands intertwined in every part of my being. The raw beauty of my body emerged before me as I nursed with sore breasts and felt a growing strength as I swayed a sleepy baby in my arms.

My face now exuded something different. Youthful flippancy replaced with reverence. Eyes crinkled when I smiled. Lines deepened on my forehead when I frowned.

Motherhood revealed to me that God had created me with a miraculous love. I learned to have a sense of reverence for my body. I learned of its God-given dignity, which is more powerful than shame, more powerful than everything.

Do you recognize your beloved dignity? Can you see God's abundant love for you in His gaze within the hue of your eyes? Maybe you hear His voice delighting in yours when you cry out to Him. Perhaps you deeply desire to feel this way, but, like me, it seems your sin has separated you, devalued you, cast you aside. Sometimes the critical voices of the culture persuade us to wrap our value within our physical appearance or our abilities or our past mistakes.

In today's scripture, Saint Paul wrote, "For I am convinced that [nothing] will be able to separate us from the love of God in Christ Jesus our Lord" (Romans 8:38–39). Reflect upon a moment when you felt unlovable and allow the truth in today's scripture to heal that wound. Through Him you conquer all. Nothing can separate you from the love of God.

As women, we face an onslaught of lies about who we truly are, many of them aimed at how we are perceived by others. However, in his letter to the Romans, Saint Paul pushes against this deception. He lists out every conceivable thing that we feel could threaten our relationship with the Lord and proclaims that none of it can.

Christ's love for us is beyond all of it, covering the brokenness of a world that demands we look a certain way. The love of God covers our past trauma and restores us. The love of God is without measure.

READING: ROMANS 8:37–39

- Think on a healing rite of passage for you, one that could have been or was challenging, but that felt redeemed. What did you learn about yourself through it?
- During a time of transition in your life, was anyone instrumental in being a mirror of God's love for you? Pray a prayer of thanksgiving for that person.

You are being rooted and grounded in love. Ephesians 3:17

LIVING IN RESTORATION

School

T he smell of incense filled the church. Glowing candles cast a soft light on the wooden pews. I gazed up at the crucifix and attempted to steady my hands. It was an exquisite carving of splintered thorns upon Christ's head with crimson stains depicting His wounds. On the opposite wall was a painting of Saint Augustine, weeping in a lush garden.

I exhaled and opened the confessional door. Silence, then a faint rustling as the priest cleared his throat and spoke in his Ugandan accent, "In the name of the Father, and the Son, and the Holy Spirit." I fumbled clumsily with the pamphlet labeled, "How to Go to Confession."

I told the priest that I had not been to confession in several years, but He nodded knowingly. I began confessing my sins. My throat constricted with each word. Tears rolled down my face as I unraveled my tangled broken mess. I gathered the debris of a shameful past and sorrowfully presented each transgression.

At last, I waited, expecting chastisement for my iniquities. Instead, compassion radiated from his deep brown eyes. Words of mercy fell from his lips. As he raised his hand to give the blessing and absolution, forgiving all of my sins, a jubilant smile spread across his face.

When I left the church, I stood outside admiring the setting sun, a tapestry of rich color, swirls of orange and pink. I thought of that painting of Saint Augustine, a terrible sinner who became a great saint. As my tears dried, peace flooded my heart.

Here, in this place, the mystery of grace was slightly uncovered. I had carried the crushing burden of my sins, the agony of my woundedness bearing down upon my weary bones with a force I could not withstand. Remorse had hung heavily on my heart. I desired redemption, but doubted it was available to a sinner like me.

I was far too shattered for whole restoration with too many polluted pieces to be washed clean. Doubt hovered over me like a shadow. My heart was uneasy and questioned whether the light of grace could reach me.

Yet, as I timidly approached the mercy of God, cowering in fear and uncertainty, I was met with love. This love surpassed all I had known about forgiveness; it reached into the depths of my captive soul and set me free. And in this freedom bought by the sacrifice of Christ, surrender was all that was asked of me. I plunged into the generous love of God, shed the garment of shame, and allowed the Lord to wrap me in His love.

His love came to me in the form of a wise and humble priest who witnessed to me the love of God, who rejoiced alongside me as my doubt was replaced with faith. In the quiet of the confessional, on holy and sacred ground, His love abided. Love had rescued me.

Maybe you are in a place of uncertainty. Afraid to approach Jesus. Unsure what will happen when you invite Him into the hidden places of your heart, into the areas of your life where you feel depleted or unsteady on your feet. Today's scripture declares that we are being "rooted and grounded in love" (Ephesians 3:17). We are firmly planted in the love of Christ. As beloved daughters we are not bound by our imperfections, enslaved to the sins of our past or present struggles, but grounded in a love that can heal us completely.

In his letter to the Ephesians, Saint Paul unveils for us the extent of God's love. He writes, "I pray that you may have the power to comprehend . . . and to know the love of Christ that surpasses knowledge, so that you may be filled with all the fullness of God" (vv. 18–19).

Sister, sometimes we place our own human limitations on Jesus. We attempt to hide these painful areas in our hearts from Him, worrying that He will not fill them with His grace. We hunger for His love, but we hold back, afraid that He will not nourish us.

We must remember that Jesus does not offer us scarcity but fullness. You do not have to hold anything back from Him. He can hold it all.

READING: EPHESIANS 3:17–19

- How we learn about and encounter God's love is often through others. For whom in your life can you be this light of love?
- Dismiss the lie that you are too far removed from God and seek His forgiveness in the sacrament of confession. Take time to turn your heart to the presence of God in this moment of your life.

The Spirit helps us in our weakness.

Romans 8:26

WEEK 26

LEGACY OF FAITH

Family of Origin

I watched the rising and falling of my grandfather's chest, his breathing ragged, fleeting, edging closer to the moment of eternal life. The holy oil from the sacrament of anointing of the sick earlier that day gleamed in between his forehead wrinkles with his salt and pepper hair meticulously combed above, as usual.

Yet nothing was usual because we were losing him. I would no longer hear his bellowing laugh. I would no longer see him reverently pause before the crucifix hanging on our wall, remove his hat, and move his lips in silent prayer. No more stories from his childhood, his smile and eyes sparkling as he shared.

A summer thunderstorm raged outside of the hospice room. Flashes of lightning appeared, winds whipped the rain through the trees. I slipped my hand into his hand, calloused from years of strumming the guitar and hard labor. *You would have loved this storm.*

The prayers of our family grew louder, and his breathing grew quieter. And then he was gone. As I glanced at the fallen faces around me and heard the laments of this immense loss, I felt the gentle voice of Jesus whisper in my heart, *Take courage, daughter.*

My grandfather's words of wisdom constantly echoed in my mind, and his life was a witness of what it meant to rely upon the Lord. My grandfather was the glue that held us all together. I learned from him to embrace the fullness of life.

When he passed away, I expected a tremendously broken heart, an irreparable severing, like a tree branch that snapped and fell to the ground. But instead, I experienced a powerful infusion of grace, lovingly lavished upon me from the heart of Christ. It was a grace that held me tightly through my grief and gave me strength. It was a gift from God.

I was blessed with the understanding that my grandfather truly had left us with a legacy of faith that would see us through it all. I would not be overwhelmed by the weight of his absence. Rather, my heart was moved to a greater sense of love, compassion, and peace.

None of it was my own resilience. All of it was a tender mercy from the Lord. I experienced pain, but that pain brought forth a richer desire to seek Jesus, rootedness that emboldened me to be like my grandfather and rely upon the Lord.

Sister, I am sure you have experienced grief and sorrow. Maybe it was the loss of a loved one, or the loss of a dream, or a sense of purpose. You might be struggling even to pray. At times, we feel unseen and unheard, even overwhelmed. This feeling of weakness is as though we are endlessly wandering in search of solid ground.

Today's scripture reminds us of the truth: "We do not know how to pray as we ought, but that very Spirit intercedes with sighs too deep for words" (Romans 8:26). We are not alone even when we feel lonely.

Even when our prayers feel dry and empty, we have the help of the Holy Spirit pouring out the living water of Christ and quenching our thirst for wholeness. Christ replenishes us in our weakness and provides for us a place within His heart to rest.

You are His beloved daughter, and He will bear fruit in your life. Scripture goes on to tell us, "We know that all things work together for good for those who love God, who are called according to his purpose" (v. 28). I invite you to let this truth restore strength in your heart.

He is with you. Christ is calling you, and even if you don't know what that purpose is yet, He continues to beckon you forward in love. His hand continues to work in your life and lead you to a deeper relationship with Him. His grace is plentiful, and He will be generous with it. You will be given every single drop of His love for you; nothing will be lost.

Rely upon Him and follow with fervor as He goes before you, joyfully anticipating the goodness He has prepared for you.

READING: ROMANS 8:26–28

- Are you experiencing spiritual dryness or richness right now in your prayer life? Remember that Jesus calls us in times of sorrow and consolation. Trust in His love today.
- Approach Scripture with fresh eyes today and ask Jesus to help you pray if you're struggling to find the words.

"Where I am going, you cannot come."

John 13:33

WEEK 27
MY TIME OF VULNERABLE NEED
Friendship

I rummaged through the growing stack of unpaid bills on our kitchen counter. My husband's paycheck from his temporary place of employment barely made ends meet after he lost his job.

Dinner simmered on the stove, remnants from the refrigerator improvised into soup. My baby let out a raspy cough and rested her feverish forehead against my cheek. I sighed and wet a washcloth with cold water. As I sang softly into her ear, my toddler dumped out a bucket of wooden blocks, sending them clattering across the floor. The baby startled and cried. I felt my own hot tears sting my eyes, but wiped them away when my preschooler stood in front of me, waving a paper. She proudly held up her drawing before dropping her crayon and turning to play with her sibling.

I heard a gentle knock at the door and pushed my hair out of my face in an attempt to look presentable. As I opened the door, a dear friend wrapped one arm around me while presenting a bag of groceries in the other.

Her smile was accentuated by the soft lines around her eyes. She listened lovingly, without a hint of judgment, as I unloaded my worries. Out of love, she entered the messy moment of my life and offered me a tender place to land.

Her authenticity brought the peace my heart was aching for. It would have been easier to hide behind a forced smile, to say that everything was fine. Easier to allow the tightness in my chest to remain concealed, every feeling heavily guarded by a wall of shame. I struggled with the desire to appear in control but the stronger desire to be accepted and loved in my difficult moment won out.

The gift of her friendship brought down all the barriers and permitted me to be real. Jesus showed up in the form of a friend with a bag full of groceries.

As we spoke, I was reminded of how much God loves us and how we are called to love others. Through my friend, I was reminded that in every hour of our day, Jesus invites us to rest in His arms, to share our burdens, and to step out of our hiding places into the light of His love.

Maybe you are like my friend, loving others in their time of need. Or maybe you are more like me, in need of the reminder that you are beloved, in need of an opportunity to be real without the looming shadow of inadequacy silencing you.

The fear that we are unlovable in our weakest moments can cause us to ignore the lump in our throat, to blink back the tears, and to constantly put on a brave face.

Yet we do not have to disguise our heartaches. Jesus welcomes us like a tenderhearted friend, wiping our tears and our mess. Sometimes we cannot see His presence amid the struggles of everyday life.

But when we strain our eyes and open our hearts, His love unfolds before us through our friendships, others' acts of mercy, our giving and sharing. Today's scripture reminds us that Jesus said, "I give you a new commandment, that you love one another. Just as I have loved you, you also should love one another" (John 13:34). Let us reflect on that calling to love as Christ loves.

This message should astound us because Christ laid down His life for us, showing us the type of love He desires us to have for each other: a sacrificial love that sees the person before us as beloved just as we are beloved. Jesus is calling us to step out in love.

Sister, I encourage you to simply show up. You lay your life down when you show up in the little, quiet moments. As beloved daughters, we are given the grace to keep showing up. Even when it is hard. Even when it is messy.

Show up for the friend who is hurting. Show up before the Lord and allow Him to reveal to you all the ways you are loved, and all the ways you can love others.

READING: JOHN 13:33–35

- Who has taught you by her example how to step into tender places of love during crises? Pay attention in order to do this for others today.
- If someone has not shown up for you when you were undergoing hardship, bring that pain to the Lord and ask for an opportunity to show His love to someone else.

He heals the broken hearted, and binds up their wounds. Psalm 147:3

WEEK 28

GROWING OUR FAMILY IN PEACE

Romantic Relationship

The altar was covered in Easter lilies. I admired the white petals, fully blooming and carrying their sweet scent throughout the church. They offered tangent symbols of purity and new life. It was the eve of Divine Mercy Sunday. The golden sun had begun to dip below the horizon sending vibrant colors through the stained glass windows.

It was my wedding day. A mere twenty years old, I knelt in prayer next to my equally young husband beneath the crucifix at the front of the church. The voice of the priest drew my eyes upward as he held Christ in the form of the Blessed Sacrament at the consecration. *This is my Body, which will be given up for you.*

I looked down at my growing belly, clearly visible beneath the lace of my wedding dress. My husband smiled at the sound of our one-year-old playfully squirming around on the church pews. Our life together had started with much brokenness.

Yet on this day, shame did not invade my heart. My wounds were healed by the tender hands of my Savior. Words of repentance in confession had spilled from my lips, and through His Holy Church they had been accepted. As we stood up, I noticed a painting of the Divine

Mercy image. One of Jesus' wounded hands was raised in blessing, the other revealed a heart pouring forth blood and water. His mercy would make all things new.

Lust poorly disguised as true affection had loomed in my relationships. My husband and I had fallen into these same sins. I had tender scars from deep wounds and baggage from past relationships. Heavy burdens left empty crevices in my heart that ached to be filled with authentic love.

One day, we returned to the Church. Tentatively pushing open the doors and stepping into a wave of peace that we had abandoned for far too long, I learned about love at the foot of the cross. Lapping up the truth of the gospel like a parched wanderer, I tried to place Jesus at the center of our family where He could become the solid foundational rock. Christ would anchor me, and I would be bound to His mercy, not my mistakes. Fear would finally flee, and I could face the painful places of our relationship and allow Jesus to heal us.

Some moments of our journey we felt crippled and stumbled, but with prayer and open hearts we approached our wedding day with tremendous hope. We stood on the altar having done the mending work of asking for healing. Our hearts were prepared to receive the grace of the sacrament of marriage. Love blossomed like the Easter lilies, full, pure, and renewed.

As we delve into today's scripture, I invite you to ponder the places of woundedness in your own heart. Maybe you are single and have been wondering where God is leading you. You might find yourself constantly questioning your vocation and desiring clarity. Perhaps you are in a relationship and unsure about what the future holds. Or you might be married and struggling.

Allow the Lord to enter those broken places. Today's scripture tells us, "He heals the brokenhearted, and binds up their wounds" (Psalm 147:3). You can offer the Lord your broken heart with confidence that He will heal it and tend to your wounds. Trust that He will wrap them in His love and His grace will cover them like a powerful salve.

Christ does not fail to fulfill His promises, and although you may not be entirely certain where He is shepherding you, rest assured that you will find healing there. He will not leave you brokenhearted. In His greatness, He leans toward you and beckons you to rest in His embrace.

Remember that Jesus is a good shepherd and His love for you is unfailing. Jesus understands your afflictions. And in His mercy, He continues to walk alongside you, desiring to fill every empty place in your heart and to soothe every ache. Let Him lead you to the place He has lovingly prepared for you. Your heart will be made whole.

READING: PSALM 147:3–5

- If you are struggling to believe relationship challenges can improve, take heart from the week's story and ask the Lord for grace to make the right choices.
- Ask the Holy Spirit to infuse you with trust that your broken heart can be healed, whatever scars and disappointments you have experienced.

There is one body and one spirit. Ephesians 4:4

WEEK 29

THE MESSY HEARTH OF MY HOME

Workplace

I bent down to kiss their foreheads and inhaled the vanilla scent of their freshly washed hair. Six little children scrubbed clean. A ring of dirt in the bathtub . . . evidence of their playtime of swinging from the tree branch in our yard while bits of loose bark rained down upon them. I glanced down at their bedroom floor and sighed. The mess of scattered toys would have to wait until tomorrow.

Then I made my way to the living room and noticed all our home imperfections: tiny handprints covering unwashed windows; a dining room table with knicks, indentations, and specks of paint; laundered sheets piled in the hallway, originally to be folded, instead made into forts. All were reminders of a house bursting at the seams with our large family, filled to the brim with our movements.

I walked to the kitchen and stood at the sink filled with a stack of dirty dishes. I watched their little hands buried deep in soap suds, working hard to impress me. They tried their best to clean them and came to me teary-eyed when they accidentally cracked a plate down the middle. I assured them that this cracked plate would bring me joy.

I would forever be reminded that this mundane, everyday work does make a difference in my journey toward holiness, that these simple acts of love are seen by God. And when I mess up and run to Him teary-eyed, He looks at me with a smile.

When I became a wife and mother, the aim for perfection poured lies into my ears about what my home should look like. Noisy demands clanged around in my head. The initial expectations and admonitions I foisted on my family were burdensome because their purpose was shallow.

I wanted a home that I could boast about, a gleaming spectacle to be shown to others. Then in His mercy, the Lord made it clear to me that my home was to be rooted in love. Every crumb swept would be offered to Jesus and magnified into something beautiful for His glory. Every meal cooked would be blessed and shared. This holy work would be done together, in many ways with many hands, and all of it would be made sacred. Half-folded laundry might be left behind to put a bandage on a scraped knee. Tiny footprints might leave their mark across a recently mopped floor. Spills would be wiped again and again. Walls would be patched. Frayed curtains would be mended. Backyards would be seeded and cared for as we sweat beneath the blazing sun. Tedious, simple work.

Yet, the fullness of this work is a great gift from the Lord and a chance to strive for holiness.

Sister, I offer you this truth: the humble work before you is blessed. Whether you work in an office and feel that you are shuffling through paperwork or are on your feet all day wiping tables and taking orders. Whether stocking shelves or running errands, rocking babies or tenderly caring for an elderly parent, all of it is holy work.

These hidden acts are set before the Father, and the love that compels you to do them with care and intention is a grace. Today's scripture tells us to "lead a life worthy of the calling to which you have been called, with all humility and gentleness, with patience, bearing with one another in love" (Ephesians 4:1–2). I invite you to reflect upon how meaningful your life is as you love the people whom God has brought before you: the child who needs a hug, the neighbor who needs a smile, the coworker who needs your advice, the spouse who needs encouragement. You are called to love these people on this day.

Find the face of Christ within these people. Through your gift of self, they may find the face of Christ within you. Seek to uncover the ways each little thing you do throughout the day can sanctify you and bring you joy. Allow the Lord to delight in your littleness. Passionately embrace your call to holiness.

In the ordinary moments of life, His extraordinary love leads you.

READING: EPHESIANS 4:1–6

- Does your daily work look differently than you had expected? Which everyday task can you bring before God as an offering?
- If the people you are surrounded by during the day challenge you, think about one concrete way you can change your perspective.

We, who are many, are one body in Christ. Romans 12:5

WEEK 30
THE BLENDED TONES
OF OUR PRAYER
Church Community

S ounds of laughter and conversation came from every corner. The savory scent of Polish dumplings, bathed in butter and simmering on the stove, drifted from the kitchen. My friend stood in her apron, cooking joyfully, with bits of fine flour in her hair.

A table was pushed against the wall, adorned with various foods and a large tray of cookies rapidly disappearing as our children snuck them away. A wicker basket filled with colorful rosaries caught the rays of sunlight beaming through the windows. Across the room a priest prepared for a house blessing, while a toddler playfully tugged at his black cassock.

When he was ready to pray, our families gathered in the modest living room. We all chuckled when he walked past me with incense and my baby coughed. Then we sat together and prayed the rosary. Smaller children joined us for brief moments and then ran off to play, swinging their rosaries behind them. The older children led us in the various mysteries, and our hearts were overjoyed at the harmony of their high-pitched voices followed by our lower adult ones.

As I looked across the room at everyone who was part of this group dedicated to praying the rosary, I noticed my little boy planting a kiss on his sister's Our Lady of Guadalupe doll. Smiling, I thought of Our Lady's words to Saint Juan Diego, "I am your merciful mother, to you, and to all the inhabitants on this land and all the rest who love me."

In this community of friends, we grew into a deeper understanding of the Lord's great love for us. Several young families, engaged couples, single people, and people discerning religious life all joined in prayer. People with diverse backgrounds and different gifts. Some of us were stay-at-home mothers; others were involved in ministry; still others were teachers. Yet we all gathered with the same desire: to love the Lord and be holy. We opened our homes and our hearts.

Through prayer requests and deep discussions around the table, I saw us as a reflection of the Catholic Church. We were brought together by the tender and motherly heart of Our Lady and a desire to be faithful. Faith is a grace-filled place where our hearts are intertwined. These were my people. The holy friendships made here lifted us closer to the love of God through prayer and encouragement. Truth was spoken in love, and the gospel looked to for guidance. In these things, Christ's Church was visibly at work. His Body was made manifest in their bold fervor for what was good and sacred.

We would share life together and see families grow, vocations revealed, and sacraments received. We would witness a blessed fellowship of both rejoicing and sometimes lamenting. This common worship from varied souls is pleasing to the Lord.

It could be that your own heart longs for gathering. Maybe you long for a community where you can come as you are and be received with love and compassion. Or you may find yourself seeking friends who will inspire your faith life, friends who will hold you accountable in ways that are wise and loving. A prayerful group of diverse people might be what your heart is aching for.

Sister, I come before you in confidence that if this is what your heart desires, the Lord will make a path for you. I know it can be challenging to step out in search of a community where you can grow and feel welcome. Prayerfully ask the Lord and Our Blessed Mother to guide you.

Today's scripture tells us, "For as in one body we have many members, and not all the members have the same function, so we, who are many, are one body in Christ" (Romans 12:4–5). The beautiful truth is that each of our gifts and our differences are necessary in the Church. We desire community because, as one body in Christ, we are seeking to glorify our beloved Jesus collectively.

Each of us has a purpose and each of us has a unique way of loving and serving the Lord. And when we share our love of Christ alongside our brothers and sisters, it is powerful. This is even more true when we go forth together and strive for holiness.

READING: ROMANS 12:4–5

- What friend can you identify whose example helps you want to grow in your love for God? Offer thanks for her presence today.
- Are you feeling a desire for community? Take these feelings to prayer and ask the Lord how He'd like you to grow community.

We believe the love that God has for us. 1 John 4:16

WEEK 31
LEADING ME TO
MARY'S SON

Relationship with the Lord

The morning air smelled of wood burning. The clouds in the sky were the color of wet cement and hung heavy with the promise of rain. Noticing the tremble in my fingers, my husband turned up the heater in our car, sending a blast of warmth that enveloped me and brought a rush of comfort to my tense bones. I am sure he knew that my hands were shaking from nerves and not the cold.

I was pregnant with our fifth baby after we had suffered a miscarriage with our fourth. We were headed to our ultrasound, and I was desperate to hear the sound of a heartbeat. I pulled my rosary from my pocket, feeling the smooth, worn beads in my hand. Despite the cheerful crinkle around his eyes as he smiled, I could tell my husband was nervous as well. His jaw tensed in between the silent movements of his lips as he gripped the steering wheel. He was praying too.

When we arrived at the office, I was greeted by a large painting of the Blessed Mother with her delicate hands on her womb and blue veil flowing from her head. I felt the Lord's gentle whisper in my heart, *Emmanuel.* At that moment I knew all would be well. As the ultrasound began, I saw the heartbeat before I heard it. A beautiful flicker in the darkness. Life. Our very own miracle.

After our loss, I worried that we would not have any more children. Fear clung to me. Crippling anxiety overwhelmed my grieving heart and planted weeds of lies in my soul. Lies that God was not with me, that He did not hear my prayers.

One day, I felt the urge to reach for my rosary. I prayed. I searched through the Word, my Bible fraying at the edges as I read the same verses numerous times to plant seeds of hope and truth in my spirit, seeds that would blossom and grow into a deeper relationship with my Savior. In His great love, God allowed me a peek into the wonder of His ways.

My son was born on the Feast of the Assumption of Mary. I found out I was expecting on the Feast of Our Lady of Guadalupe. And that cold January day, when the flicker of his strong heartbeat twinkled on the screen, was the Feast of the Solemnity of Mary, Mother of God. My faith increased swiftly in that moment as Jesus had given me the tender love of His mother when I was longing for it.

Our Lady did what she always does: she led me right to her Son. Then He showed me His glory and that everything is held in His mighty hands. His love for me was displayed profoundly. God was with me through it all.

You may have gone through times when you felt that God was far from you. Maybe you are in this place right now, reaching your hands out and pleading with the Lord to come closer. If you find yourself in this difficult place, struggling with prayer and searching for His voice amid all the noise, I encourage you to lean into today's scripture: "God abides in those who confess that Jesus is the Son of God, and they abide in God. So we have known and believe the love that God has for us. God is love, and those who abide in love abide in God, and

God abides in them" (1 John 4:15–16). Let this verse rest in your heart. Repeat it so that it becomes a familiar friend during challenging times.

This scripture tells us that God is always with us. Even when you think He is far away and you are seeking His face, His gentle breath is whispering love over you. His face will be right next to yours. God is intimate and ever so close to you because you are His beloved daughter.

Stand in this truth and be assured by it. Proclaim His love for you with a boldness that does not waiver despite the ever-changing conditions around you. God does not change; His love remains steadfast; and the Light of the World is generous with His love. Open your heart and receive it. You are His beloved daughter, and He abides in you.

READING: 1 JOHN 4:15–16

- Have you experienced consolation directly from Jesus or from His mother? Or perhaps God sent someone else. Walk through that memory.
- Consider adopting a new prayer practice like five minutes of scripture reading a day or praying a rosary. Take a step to grow in your awareness of God's presence. He's always right there beside you.

PART 4

BELIEVING

by Jenna Guizar

Set aside the myth that your self-reliance as a woman means you have to do it all on your own, in your own way, without the help or light of others. Instead, accept this invitation from the Lord to fully embrace your identity and worth as being made in His image and likeness. You will find yourself in your faith in God.

We walk through ten stories from my life, ten unique stages from early childhood through adolescence to mature adulthood, which are paired with illuminating scripture passages. We encourage you to open your Bible and follow along. Take time with the questions and let them sit inside your heart.

"This is my Son, the Beloved, with whom I am well pleased."

Matthew 3:17

WEEK 32
JESUS THERE ALL ALONG
Childhood

The room froze in my view as I watched the girls across the table whisper to each other, hands cupping their mouths so no one could make out what they were saying, all the while looking at me as they told their secrets. I heard my mom's voice in my head, *Sit up straight. Don't let them get to you.* I desperately wanted to melt into the floor and disappear. The girls giggled and looked at each other like they had just accomplished some great goal. They actually had succeeded in making me feel worthless and left behind.

My love of justice welled up inside of me and compelled me to ask, "What are you guys talking about?" Everyone eating lunch at this table knew exactly what, or whom, these girls whispered about. You could always see it in their eyes. They never learned how to shield their eyes the way they covered their mouths. The eyes were the giveaway, the gateway to knowing exactly the target of their gossip.

The kids around me started moving again, and then everything felt like a time-lapse movie, zooming so quickly I could barely make out hidden glances by other kids. I felt burning from the inside out, hot with embarrassment and anxiety.

Why were they so cruel? Why did they say such awful things about me right in front of me?

I look back at my little self and wish I had known about Jesus.

I wish I had known He was there, sitting right beside me as those little girls whispered disparaging things about me—about my body, about my looks. I wish I had known He was looking at me with immense delight, studying His creation with great affection.

I didn't know He was there all along, through every insulting whisper, every taunting glance, every rejection from my peers. So I began to believe what they whispered about me—that I was ugly, that I was too loud, that I was an outcast, that I was invisible.

And these thoughts clung to the insecurity inside of me, building a home in my heart where the belief in my belovedness was supposed to break ground. The foundation to this home of insecurity seemed massive, able to withstand so much, building its footings inside my young heart.

The footings are hard to dig out, even these days. I wonder if it's the same for you too? Even if you think you've overcome the insecurity of your past and you've knocked down that home that made a place in your heart for years. Perhaps you realize the foundation had set in deeper than you had thought. The insecurities grip your breath as your senses are heightened each time you wonder if someone is talking about you, if you are really invisible, if God even delights in you.

Spoiler alert: He does.

He delights in all of the parts of you He created: your intellect, your body, your spirit, your soul. He wants to enter into all of the pain, the wrong thoughts, the doubt—and He wants you to lay a foundation not on those things, but on Him. This foundation is strong and mighty; a foundation withstanding assaults from the Enemy; a foundation built solidly on the Holy Spirit, the Giver of Life.

He comes into our little (and big) hearts and digs out the deepest unhealthy thoughts, desires, and beliefs. He comes with the gentleness of a lover, and He slowly and surely unearths those unhealthy substructures, brings them up to the light, and breaks them down. And He invites us to lay a new foundation and to secure ourselves in the belief of who we are: daughters of the Father.

We begin building the blocks of belief in Him, the One who calls us His beloved, His creation, His daughter. We let Him in to do the work in our fragile hearts, allowing His Holy Spirit to make them His own.

And just as Jesus emerged from the water, we emerge as new women, forever changed by the God who loves us, who comes for us, who never leaves us. We place our trust in the One who calls us His own as we entrench our identity in the truth He says over us, "This is my [daughter], the Beloved, with whom I am well pleased" (Matthew 3:17).

And we will never be the same.

READING: MATTHEW 3:16–17

- What lies have taken hold in your life? What are you believing about yourself that simply isn't true in light of today's scripture?
- Think about one way you give delight to God the Father. If you are struggling, ask a trusted loved one what they think.

The people who sat in darkness have seen a great light. Matthew 4:16

CHOICES BEYOND MY REGRETS

Young Adulthood

T he vibrations of my phone woke me; my eyes tried to blink away the brightness of my friend's bedroom. I slowly rolled over to silence my phone. *It's probably my mom*, I thought, putting a pillow over my head to drown out the noise of the birds chirping outside and the fan above me. I dozed off, hoping that the next time I awoke the headache would be gone and the day wouldn't be as bright.

Finally, I decided it was probably time to wake up. Grabbing my stuff and making sure I had my sunglasses for that Arizona sun, I headed out the door and climbed into my car.

I cranked up my air conditioner to blast away the heat, and I looked in the rearview mirror. I lifted my glasses and saw my blood-shot eyes peering back at me, a reminder that last night was yet another night of overindulgence and depravity.

When would I stop giving into these temptations: alcohol, drugs, and the comfort of men? When would I stop letting the noise and distraction of the world run my life? When would I recognize that I was worth more than a night of debauchery? I put my sunglasses back on and turned the music up loud, drowning out my questions, longings, and uneasiness as I cruised onto the hot streets, heading home.

I have experienced countless nights (and mornings) like these—ones where I arose and realized how much regret I held for these actions that were so far from God's heart for me. He has more for you and me than a life filled with sorrow. He has more for you and me than squinting at the brightness of the day, only wishing to be back in the night. He has more for you and for me than a desire for darkness. He has life for you and me. He has light for you and me.

His light shines in the darkness. No matter how dark your night gets, no matter how far gone you think you are, no matter how deep in sin you may be, no matter the darkness you've experienced from others, His light shines even there. And for each one of us who has sat in darkness for hours, days, months, or years, light is dawning. It is breaking through the darkness, coming for you and for me.

Here is where we are invited to a decision. Here is where we choose to take off our sunglasses that have kept us in the dark for so long and allow that light to come into our souls and the shadowy places of our hearts. Instead of running away from the light, covering it up with pillows over our heads and blackout shades on our windows and sin in our hearts, we can choose to let Him in.

We see in the scripture a callback to the prophet Isaiah: "Light has dawned" (Matthew 4:16). And with this Light, Jesus, we have clear vision. We see who we are in Our Father's eyes: children of the Light. We were made for Light. Whatever darkness has been put on us, from others, from ourselves, from the world, let us lift our faces to the One who has dawned.

We can see a great Light and a new beginning. We can see a future with hope because we have a God who has come into all darkness and shone His magnificent Light.

Jesus invites us here into this lifelong journey, and our first step is one of repentance: "Repent, for the kingdom of heaven has come near" (v. 16). We can think about when we knew in our hearts that we were turning away from God's love, and then choose to turn back to Him and see His merciful heart, even in the darkest of moments.

And so we overcome darkness with the power of the Light of the World because darkness cannot overcome Him. Darkness has no place here where the Light breaks through. He's breaking through all the shadow places and saying, "There is healing, hope, and light for this."

The Light of the World wants to reside in your heart. This is what we were made for. Let us believe it today.

READING: MATTHEW 4:16–17

- Where in your life does God desire to shed light? Which habits do you want to step away from, believing you are worth more than where they lead you?
- If you have struggled to go to the sacrament of confession, find a time at a parish near you or make an appointment this week. Believe God desires this healing for you.

◇

He had come
from God
and was
going to God.

John 13:3

WEEK 34
LEADING LIKE
THE LORD

Rite of Passage

I started researching website themes on my laptop. I loved to test themes and what they could do, look like, and offer the end user. A few hours later I had landed on a perfect theme needing minimal tweaking by me. I figured this was the right next step: get a website up.

Only a day prior I had reached out to some women I knew through a Catholic Blogging Facebook group, and I had already heard back from a handful of them with an excited *yes* to the idea of starting a new Catholic women's ministry with me. I had searched for a while to find something Catholic comparable to the beautiful Protestant ministries that focused on a love of scripture, but I had come up empty.

Every time I got a "Yes, sounds great!" in my inbox, I was shocked. First of all, they were saying *yes* to something that 1) didn't have a name, and 2) didn't necessarily have a clear vision. But they were "in," so I figured it was time to make a website. Those were the easy parts: asking Catholic women to begin writing daily reflections and tinkering with websites.

The harder parts began when I realized that now I was a leader, because I had a lot of growing to do when it came to leadership.

I had had bouts of influence as captain of most of my high school sports teams, but that's where the leadership opportunities began and ended. I never sought out leadership positions at work; in fact, I preferred being a part of the crowd, going with the flow of what the CEO or boss told us to do, being a follower (and working hard while doing so). I never dreamed of being in charge.

And yet the Lord continued to inspire me. He continued to nudge me, inch by inch, to keep moving forward with this Catholic community for which I so desperately yearned myself. So I've simultaneously grown with this community of women, one step at a time, falling at times and having to apologize, and getting back up to learn all over again.

I've realized leadership doesn't mean reading every best-selling book on the topic. As I've read through scripture, I've come to understand that the best leader to learn from is Jesus Christ Himself. He shows me how to be humble, how to pray, how to discern, how to navigate conflict, and more through His life in scripture.

But most of all, He has taught me the most important characteristic of leadership: being a servant. That means, above all else, humility, generosity, kindness, and mercy reign. Love reigns.

In the scripture for today, we read that Jesus "got up from the table, took off his outer robe, and tied a towel around himself. Then he poured water into a basin and began to wash the disciples' feet and to wipe them with the towel that was tied around him" (John 13:4–5).

Jesus showed us how to put ourselves aside, get down on our knees, and wash each other's feet. He taught us that to lead means to lay down your own life and give generously to your people. He modeled for us how to believe in our identity from the Lord and humbly serve those in our lives. The God of the Universe did this, for you and for me. And so, it is our call to do as He did, to love as He loved.

This isn't just for people working in the Church; this is for everyone. He is asking us to learn from His model of servant leadership and give up our lives in service to others.

How does this resonate with your life, sister? Who is present in your life today whom you can care for with a servant's heart?

In this humble servant leadership, in this humble posture, we overcome our insecurity and embody who Christ calls us to be: women on fire with His love and Holy Spirit, opening our arms in service and in love.

READING: JOHN 13:3–5

- Think of a time when you were called to lead. Would you have done it differently from the perspective of being a servant leader?
- Where does reluctance hold you back from believing you are called to serve the people in front of you? Bring that to the Lord in prayer.

Approach the throne of grace with boldness. Hebrews 4:16

❧ WEEK 35 ❧

SETTING MYSELF BY HIS STANDARDS

School

I caught the corner of my suitcase on the edge of my nightstand. "Jenna, be careful with your stuff! Don't scratch your things up!" my mom called to me as she left to empty the car.

I sighed, since not a whole lot mattered to me. Back at home after just one year of college. *What a failure*, I scolded myself. I sat on my bed and couldn't help but think about what everyone else would think of me: a person who couldn't even last for more than a year at college. A girl who set out to conquer the real world, and instead ended up a weak and uneducated member of society. A girl who confidently stepped into dorm life as a faithful Catholic and walked out of that same dorm hanging on for dear life, seeped in sin and struggle. My psyche played the loop round in my head: *You are a failure.*

I snapped out of it as my mom burst into the room. "Okay, sweetie! Let's get the rest of your stuff up here. Did you want to save all of your papers in this drawer? Do you know where your dad went? Come down and help me. I'm not lifting all this stuff alone." I took a breath and hunched over, sulking in this moment before I got up to help my mom carry all of my belongings back to my high school bedroom.

This feeling of being a failure creeps in regularly, reminding me that I'm not as successful or driven as some people might expect me to be. I haven't hit the worldly metrics of prosperity, still floundering in so many ways in my lack of practical wisdom. I'm not as intelligent or as prudent as others in my same state in life, and I feel judgment over my every move as I struggle through life.

I'm sure you have experienced the feelings of failure because of opinions on your education choices, what you studied, the grades you received, or some other area in which you may feel less-than. We have two options when these thoughts creep in, whether from our own minds or the Enemy's whispers: we can choose life or death. Often I find it so much easier to choose death, to fall into the pit of self-hatred, doubt in my abilities, pity at my lack of the natural gifts others seem to have.

It can be more difficult to choose life, to choose to believe what God says about us, to believe we are becoming the women He wants us to be, so long as we are abiding in Him. He is forming us to be fully surrendered to His will, unattached to the world, and wholly submitted to our Creator.

The Enemy wants nothing more than to hold us back from this trust that we belong to God and are becoming everything He desires us to be. The Enemy wants to tell us how far we have to go and tempt us to think, *Why even try?*

But we are called to try and choose life. We are invited to approach Our Father, as we hear in today's scripture reading: "Let us therefore approach the throne of grace with boldness" (Hebrews 4:16). We are daughters of the Father who desires to pour out mercy and grace into our lives, our minds, our bodies, and our souls. Why do we turn away from this invitation to boldness? Maybe we turn away because we're worried that He won't answer our requests.

But Jesus will not leave us dry and empty. He pours out and pours out and pours out. Grace upon grace. Mercy unending.

And we become the women He is forming because we believe this truth. Through all of my failures, successes, and everything in between, He is always there. And He is there for you too. Let's boldly approach His throne together, hand-in-hand, to receive the outpouring of grace and mercy, which never ends.

Be brave with me, sweet sister. Let's choose life. Let's believe. And let's be filled with grace upon grace, for this moment, for this circumstance, for this beautiful and adventurous life.

READING: HEBREWS 4:16

- Does your day include a special time for bringing your heart, hope, and hurts before Our Lord? When could you make time for this?
- Who in your life is a good example of being frank about her need for help? What can you learn from her example of believing that it is okay to not be perfect?

✧

"You will receive power when the Holy Spirit has come upon you." Acts 1:8

WEEK 36
REIGNITED FIRE
IN THE SPIRIT
Family of Origin

The first time I had ever been to my cousin's house was also the first time we ever prayed together as a family. Unlike our usual family festivities, this get-together was a hard one to attend. We were here to pray for healing over my aunt who was just diagnosed with cancer.

Everyone gathered together, fidgeting and awkwardly looking around the room. My cousin stood up, the eldest granddaughter of fourteen, cleared her throat and said, "Thank you for coming."

And one by one, each of us shared a heartfelt word with my aunt, reminding her we would be there for her every step of the way: she wouldn't be alone, she was fierce, she was a fighter. With each person's words, we cried tears of sorrow and even tears of joy.

My second-eldest cousin reminisced about the first time he went to church with my aunt. He shared what a gift it was to witness her heart fall in love with the Lord. I was struck by the effect of my aunt's witness, the testimony of a newly revived Christian heart repenting and letting her heart be transformed by Jesus. Her witness gave him a chance to see the Lord's grace anew, even though he had walked with the Lord his whole life. And because of seeing her life change, he fell in love with the Lord again.

How many times does the Lord's grace want to fall afresh on us through the witness of a family member or a friend? The witnessing of that person may even happen because we tell them about Christ's life, death, and resurrection or we surrender to the Holy Spirit's promptings to invite them in. And in this beautiful cycle of witnessing, the Body of Christ continues to be made new.

This is what it means to be a witness "in all Judea and Samaria, and to the ends of the earth" (Acts 1:8)—even, and especially, in our families. We are given the command to be His witnesses to the ends of the earth. Even in a cancer diagnosis, even in an unknowable future, we are invited to be His witnesses.

My own heart was changed after this story. I felt a renewed longing for intimacy and relationship with our God who offers mercy to each one of us. And most especially, I walked away from that night with a heart on fire to be a witness.

I want to witness by living a life in step and on fire with the power of the Holy Spirit who would testify to my family, friends, and coworkers. I want to share a God who desires to know each one of them, a Creator who longs to be in relationship with them, a Holy Spirit who lights a fire in their bones and brings them to life.

Jesus promised this Holy Spirit when He said, "You will receive power when the Holy Spirit has come upon you" (v. 8), and His promises do not fail. We trust the promises of Our Lord, and He has given us power to live a life of faith, surrendered and made new by the God of the Universe.

This is for you too. You were made to give witness to the Holy Spirit to your family and your friends and every person in your life. Not every witness looks the same. Not every witness is flashy and loud, exciting or emotionally stirring. We can live a quiet life of witness, sharing through our example and everyday lives. Maybe we extend just one simple invitation to a rosary, to Mass, to Eucharistic Adoration. But believe that God is both calling you and empowering you to be His witness. Trust in that truth.

Ask the Lord, *To whom do You desire me to witness?* The scripture today encourages us, "You will receive power when the Holy Spirit has come upon you" (v. 8). He is ready and poised to work through you in your life. The question is, will you let Him?

Let's overcome our fears and step into the power He's given us. It is what we were made for.

READING: ACTS 1:8

- Who has given witness to the saving power of the Holy Spirit in your life? Say a prayer of thanksgiving for her or his example now.
- Have you or has someone in your life had a difficult health journey or diagnosis this year? Take any anger, hurt, and confusion to the Lord in prayer. Believe that He cares to hear your experience of it.

✦

Let love be genuine. Romans 12:9

WEEK 37
FROM FRIEND TO SISTER
Friendship

I t was my friend Tiffany who encouraged me to start dating my now-husband. One day she told me about this guy named Mike who was a friend of hers. She invited him over to hang out with us, and I immediately liked him.

I called her later that night. "What do you think? I think I like him." She told me, "I mean, he's ready to get married," thinking it might make me back off.

"Sounds good to me," I replied.

A few years later, I was at a crossroads in life. Mike and I were married, I was pregnant, and he was a drummer in a worship band. We had very little money, and it was time for me to look into a career.

Tiffany had been a respiratory therapist for years, so she prompted me to drive over to the local trade school for medical professionals. They told me the nursing program had a two-year wait list, but that their respiratory therapy program started in two weeks. I signed right up.

So much has changed in the last twelve years! We have different jobs, have been blessed with more children, and have mourned a few miscarriage losses. My friendship with Tiffany has grown closer because she married my brother. A close friendship is now a family affair.

My spiritual director has invited me to start noticing God's patterns in my life, and I can see one with Tiffany. She introduced me to my husband; she introduced me to my first career; she has walked alongside so much of my journey with Blessed is She; and she is one of my biggest cheerleaders.

She has a genuine love for me that I've oftentimes felt undeserving of, and her generosity surpasses my understanding. But most of all, she's patient with me when I'm not very thoughtful about how I may have hurt her or how I've offended her or my brother with my choices. She outdoes me because she knows how to love.

Her example of mercy and kindness has covered over a gaping hole in my heart: one that I let fester because I believed that if I'm not enough for someone, if I'm not the right kind of friend, if I'm not meeting expectations, I'll be left behind. I've always thought there isn't enough patience to deal with someone like me. But Tiffany shows me there is by showing me true friendship and authentic love.

And it makes me want to genuinely love not only her, but each of my friends. Her example is Jesus to me, and I want to be Jesus to another friend.

Our scripture for today reminds us how to be a loving friend: "Let love be genuine; hate what is evil, hold fast to what is good" (Romans 12:9). This is what friendship looks like: loving with a genuine heart, holding fast to the good in friendships, and letting go of what is evil.

Sometimes it can be hard to find friendships like this. If that's how it is for you right now, I invite you to be gentle with yourself. Instead of believing it is because you aren't good enough—as a friend, sister, family member, employee—consider that perhaps the people in your life need you to be this example to them.

Don't let insecurities fester in your heart. We all have growing to do, and the Lord will help you to grow as fast as you can, in His will and timing.

He is patient with you and loves you and always will. We have a friend in Christ even if we can't find a friend who loves us right here and right now. Sometimes we start those friendships by being this kind of friend.

Consider who in your life you could reach through genuine love and mutual affection. Which relationships need time, effort, and some prayer to become closer to this holy kind of friendship?

And you know what's fun? Some friends, they just might become your sisters.

READING: ROMANS 12:9–10

- If you're feeling dry in friendship right now, go back through your memories and be comforted or inspired to do more for others.
- Look for the patterns of friendship in your life and talk them over with a trusted confidante. Strive to be aware and cultivate healthy friendships.

Love one another. 1 John 4:7

WEEK 38
MY ADVOCATE
FOR GRACE
Romantic Relationship

My husband's confidence is probably the most attractive thing about him. His presence and stature command a room, a dinner table, even a football field. His confidence doesn't stop with himself—he believes in me too. And I know he would believe in you too if he knew you. He believes in people in a way I've never seen. He doesn't see your circumstances or your past or your sins; he sees the person you were created to be.

As a nineteen-year-old girl reading books on atheism, I remember the first time his confidence overwhelmed me. I was in the doorway of his home, asking him what he was up to that day, wondering if we were going to grab something to eat or wait for his roommates to come home. I told him about this book I had been reading, and how it had me questioning everything I had previously believed in.

"There can't be a God," I said, quoting the book. "This world has to just be happenstance."

He stood up from the couch, so sure, so caring, and he said, "You know that's not true. That is a lie. I want you to throw that book away, and you need to go to confession."

I looked back at him, astounded. *How do you know it's not true?* I wanted to ask. *How can you say that with such certainty?* But I didn't have to ask.

His faith was enough to get me out the door, in the car, and in front of a priest to receive Jesus' healing grace in the confessional, filling in all of the cracks the atheism book had created in my heart.

My husband's confidence has been an advocate of grace in my life. And I'm seeing how grace has moved through him in our many years of marriage. That grace is love.

This is how you love someone: be a vehicle for grace. Never hinder or become a barricade to the movement of God's grace in their lives, but instead let grace move through you. Become an open vessel from which His grace pours into and out of.

This doesn't mean being a cookie cutter of someone you think you're supposed to be like in order to be a vessel of love. We can read the lives of the saints or look at our holy friends and wish we could just emulate how they acted, how they responded. But as my husband would remind me, God wants us to be the vessel of love that only we can be, the particular vessel that's filled with God's deep love in a personalized way.

He has a story to tell with your life that He will not tell with someone else's. You were created by Love to love.

We know God sent His Son out of a deep love. He poured out His Spirit out of a deep love. Our scripture today shares, "God's love was revealed among us in this way: God sent his only Son into the world so that we might live through him" (1 John 4:9). And I see now that we must model what Our Lord did and does: be a person who pours out. We must pour out what Our Lord is putting into us: His Spirit, grace, generosity, peace, patience, charity, kindness, self-control, faithfulness, joy, and gentleness.

When we live in communion with Our Lord, we can live in the confidence of His love. We can live in the certainty of our identity as His daughters who will never run dry when loving others in our lives. We will never run dry in our families, relationships, or friendships. We will never run dry because we have a Father who is always pouring into us, and if we accept this beautiful grace, we will always have enough.

We can love because we believe in the promise of scripture: "Love one another, because love is from God" (v. 7). It's not from our own conjured-up way to love; it is from Our Lord Himself.

We can stand in the certainty of not only who we are, but what we do. We love because we have a God who loves us.

And that's what my husband would tell you, I'm sure of it.

READING: 1 JOHN 4:7–9

- What books or podcasts or social media outlets do not help you grow spiritually? Which ones are you ready to take out of your life and off your phone?
- Ask God for an increase in His love and the grace to share love more freely today with everyone you encounter. Believe He will answer your call.

✧

"Love your enemies." Luke 6:27

WEEK 39

LOVING BEYOND
SLANDER

Workplace

Years ago, I was slandered publicly on the internet. People said awful things about me and my beliefs, about my work, about what I stand for. And other people believed them.

I hung up the phone after reading the hateful words to my friend who lives across the country. She had tried to comfort me, but the situation was too big, overwhelming, and distressing. Feeling sad that her words didn't lift me, I walked into my bathroom and turned on my shower. Getting under the showerhead, I released all the tension in my body, and the flood of tears came pouring out.

I cried tears for every awful word this person said about me. I cried tears for the people who believed her. I cried tears for the pit in my stomach that made me think, *How could someone actually believe all that?*

The experience brought so much pain, self-doubt, and confusion. Self-doubt in what I was doing online cultivating the community of Blessed is She and about my pure and transparent heart for others. Confusion about my ability to trust others and how someone could treat me so poorly and have little to no regard for my feelings, my family, my faith.

And yet, as painful as it was, it did not discourage me from my work spreading God's teachings, especially on love.

Despite that situation, I still believe in people, redemption, and mercy because of Our Lord Jesus Christ. In today's scripture, Jesus is very specific: "Love your enemies, do good to those who hate you, bless those who curse you, pray for those who abuse you" (Luke 6:27–28). Our Lord Himself teaches us that even if someone hates us, we still love her. Even when someone curses us, we still pray for her and bless her.

I believe when Jesus Christ commanded this, He meant a soul-surrendering sort of love. One that doesn't make sense, is contrary to every instinctual feeling. This kind of love means that even if someone were to try to harm your heart . . . you would love her. *Lord, if that's not one of the hardest commandments You've ever said, I don't know what is.* Loving her means treating her with dignity even when it is painful to do.

I've come to understand that loving someone doesn't always mean letting him or her in your life over and over again to potentially cause you more harm. If we are in a position of danger, we absolutely should get out of the situation and pray for and bless someone from afar.

Sister, Jesus knows about that suffering you or someone close to you may have gone through or is currently going through. And He is with you in that pain. He will never leave or forsake you.

Even when (not if) someone hurts you—in your workplace, in your families, in your friendships—you are invited to treat them as you would have them treat you, just as Jesus commands us today in Luke 6:31.

But He doesn't stop there. His commands are actualized in His life and death. He isn't asking us to do something He Himself isn't willing to do. He demonstrated that on the cross. He showed us what it costs to "love [our] enemies" (v. 27). Jesus gave His life even for those enemies who crucified Him. He lived in the freedom of the Holy Spirit to give even in the midst of the attempt to strip Him of His dignity, His worth, His life.

And in the midst of that suffering, He freely gave for you and me. In the midst of whatever comes our way, we can listen to our Savior's commands and see how He lived His life to love as He did.

Like Him, we can lay down our lives, every single day. Like Him, we can love our enemies, bless those who curse us, and pray for those who hurt us. With Him, we can live a life of mercy.

READING: LUKE 6:27–28, 30–31

- Take a mental inventory of how you've approached being wronged at work. Are you self-righteous in your venting or condemnation of the person or his or her actions? Have you tried to approach the situation with today's scripture in mind? What would you do differently, if anything?
- Who in your life has shown you how to live out the Golden Rule? Who has treated you kindly when you didn't return the favor? Offer a prayer for these people now.

Grow up in every way into him. Ephesians 4:15

RETREAT FOR
NOURISHMENT

Church Community

About a year after Blessed is She started, I decided to host a retreat. Retreats were always a part of my faith life growing up: removing myself from the complexities of everyday life and going to a designated place for the weekend to grow and deepen my walk with the Lord.

A handful of my dear friends and I started to put it together: one friend wrote content, one helped with food, one prepared the space, one thought of speakers we could invite. Bit by bit, we used our community to bring this very first retreat to life.

At the end of the evening on the last night of the retreat, I stood at the back of the dark room and watched women kneel in front of the Blessed Sacrament, singing songs of praise to Him. I looked up at Our Lord in the monstrance and exhaled a sigh of thanksgiving. I had this beautiful realization in my heart: This was all for me. This retreat, this community of women, this beautiful moment of prayer. He was pursuing me.

I knew this was for everyone there too, of course. This whole event had been a group effort, put together piece by piece by all of us. The Lord had worked through our human efforts to create an experience that will not be forgotten. But I also felt in my bones that the Lord had brought together these friends, these people, this event in order to deepen my own personal devotion and love for Him. He desired that I would long for Him.

And because of that very first retreat and every moment of this beautiful community of women, I have found a deep love for Him in my heart that had previously been only a surface-level love. He has purified my heart when I didn't even know I needed it. He has brought me to life through this community of Catholic women, and I sit in gratitude every day for this calling He has pressed into my heart.

He has helped me grow up and will do so in ways I cannot even think of. He has put people in my life at just the right time to create more and more aspects of Blessed is She that are in His will and for His glory.

Each one of us, whether on staff with Blessed is She or a woman hosting an intimate Blessed Brunch, plays a significant part of this community's story. And it has been a gift to my heart in more ways than I could ever express.

Your journey toward community and building friendships with other Catholic women might have twists and turns in it as well, sister. I've learned that nothing grows overnight and nothing grows without pain. The Lord has a plan for your community and mine, unfolding in His time.

The Lord helps each of us to grow along with this community. Today's scripture reminds us "we must grow up in every way into him who is the head, into Christ, from whom the whole body . . . promotes the body's growth in building itself up in love" (Ephesians 4:15–16). He is joining us to each other and, most importantly, to Him.

We believe that He is the one with the knowledge of what is best for us, taking time to promote our growth. What freedom we find in this belief—trusting that God is our head, and we are along for the ride. And instead of worrying about how this will ever come to be, we can remember that this scripture is "speaking the truth in love" (v. 15). Jesus isn't condemning us that we haven't done all the growing ourselves; He simply grows us with love.

Of course, we can't do it all on our own. Just as the Holy Spirit has guided me in this work, in my own heart, in my own friendships, and in this beautiful Catholic community, He will guide you too. We can let Him in to brighten the darkness, to soften our hardened hearts, and to keep writing our story.

We are growing up into Him and will continue to do so. Let's go along for the ride.

READING: EPHESIANS 4:15–16

- How does your church community look today? Would you like for things to grow or change? Bring those to Our Lord.
- If God has placed the desire on your heart to help reach out to women to deepen friendships in your community, what is your next step? Ask the Holy Spirit to guide you.

"Power is made perfect in weakness."

2 Corinthians 12:9

WEEK 41

DEEP INTO UNION

Relationship with the Lord

I bent my body in worship, releasing my tension. I let go of the uncertainty that plagued my brain and gave way to the thoughts: *Maybe this is real. Maybe there is a Creator. Maybe He did send His Son. Maybe His Son died for me. Maybe He sent His Holy Spirit. Maybe He is everything we hoped for.*

While thinking these thoughts, tears filled my eyes, and I could not hold them in. How could our Creator love me so much that He sent His Son to die for me? What a gift, this Father who sent His Spirit to comfort me, to purify me, to remain with me always.

I lifted my eyes to see the monstrance on the altar, the light flooding in from the window, hitting it in a beautiful cascade. *You are real,* I prayed silently. *You came, died, and rose again. You reconciled me to my Father.* And as my heart filled with belief, I rose in faith and walked out into the sunlight.

The ten years before this I had struggled with atheism. I had wondered if any of it was real, if Jesus was really the Son of God, and if there even was a Creator. I had contemplated the fear that comes with the hypothesis that when we die, that is the end of it. I had battled with myself over all of the lingering questions that may always go unanswered simply because they are mysteries.

But even more than struggling and wondering, I had lived in fear of these questions I had (and felt like I would always have), preventing me from having the relationship with God that I desired. This fear made me feel like I wouldn't be able to truly long for an intimate union with God, that I was powerless to this fragility inside of me, that I would never be able to overcome my disbelief.

And I've only now come to realize, I *am* powerless. When I am trying to find the source of power with my own hands, I will always be left just shy of real, tangible healing and restoration. I will never be able to overcome this on my own. I wasn't made for self-reliance, no matter how hard I try.

What has become more apparent to me, and perhaps for you as well on your journey, is the fact that I was made for relationship, and specifically a relationship with a God who is strong in all of my weaknesses. A relationship with a God who sees all of my doubt and tells me, "I am pursuing you still." A relationship with a God who desires to answer all my questions and experience intimacy with me.

The scripture we are reflecting on today makes this clear for us: "'My grace is sufficient for you, for power is made perfect in weakness.' So, I will boast all the more gladly of my weaknesses, so that the power of Christ may dwell in me" (2 Corinthians 12:9). His power is even more magnified in my weakness. His power overcomes my weakness in ways I can never conceive. His power, especially through the grace of the sacraments, revives and renews and makes new.

His grace is sufficient. His power makes me strong. And He is making you strong too.

Whatever your weakness is, His power overcomes. And His power is made perfect in that weakness. Not in a general way—but in your specific weakness. Your self-reliance and your thought patterns that say, *I must control everything because there is no one else*, are cast aside by the perfect power of this God. But only if we let Him into our weakness, only if we surrender to His grace.

No matter what weakness we have experienced or will experience, God will pour out His grace upon us in the sacraments, in the Church, and in His word—and He will bring His power that overcomes.

So, let us not be afraid of our weakness. Let us bend in worship to Our God who overcomes and rise in belief of the power of His Holy Spirit.

READING: 2 CORINTHIANS 12:9–10

- Has your faith relationship with God felt bumpy or smooth? If you're in a time of questioning, turn your heart back to what you know about God. Ask Him to help your disbelief in prayer today.
- If you're concerned that your weaknesses will draw you away from God, get to daily Mass and receive Him in the Blessed Sacrament. His graces are real and will show you His love for you.

$$\diamond$$

PART 5

BECOMING

by Liz Kelly

Set aside the myth that your success as a woman is measured by the world's standards, by the metrics of what you "should" do or how you "should" do it. Instead, accept this invitation from the Lord to fully embrace your identity and worth as being made in His image and likeness. You will grow in virtue as you follow God's plan for your life.

We walk through ten stories from my life, ten unique stages from early childhood through adolescence to mature adulthood, which are paired with illuminating scripture passages. We encourage you to open your Bible and follow along. Take time with the questions and let them sit inside your heart.

Honor your father and mother.

WEEK 42

HONORED BY
MY MOTHER

Childhood

I was twelve, and it was the first real funeral I understood—for my classmate's infant sister.

In a postpartum psychosis, my classmate's mother said she heard a voice tell her to stab her infant daughter and throw her out the window. Her brother had found her. It was late winter, and all I could imagine was this perfect baby girl lying in a glistening, white snowbank with a shock of red blood.

After the funeral, the rest of my classmates went back to school, but I found this inconceivable. My mom came to pick me up. It was a sunny day, one that promised spring, and the snow was beginning to melt, revealing the rich, black farming soil that lay beneath it.

In our station wagon, I glanced over at my mother's gloved hands as she drove me home. She took one hand off the wheel and reached over to pat me. She said quietly, "Why don't you go for a ride when you get home." She knew this was not a time for words for me but rather a time for being and sensing. And nowhere did I feel safer as a child than with my horse, riding through the open countryside.

As the day wore on, I rode in the snow and heard the crunch that my horse's hooves made. Her name was Windy, and I found her to be an especially tenderhearted, high-strung animal. Horses like that can sense so much the emotional timbre of their rider. I swear she almost tip-toed that afternoon, so gentle was her gait.

Looking back on that day, I have come to understand that some of our wounds and hurts are so unspeakable, it's as if they need to be absorbed by the world itself. The mourning I needed to do that day was so sweeping and so incomprehensible, nothing less than the whole earth could absorb it.

And my mourning and confusion over this first confrontation with evil in my young life almost seemed to melt into the landscape—and it lays there still, buried under the soil, a child's tears and her knowledge that her understanding of the world would never be the same.

That dreadful day, my mother reverenced my sorrow and released me to the barn. She released me though she knew she could no longer protect me in the same way because I now knew a world where evil erupts with brute force. She released me to this sacred task of grieving and struggling to understand—it was not something she could do for me. And the land—it received me, just as a few hours earlier it had received that tiny casket, somber and aching with the holiness of the task with which it had been entrusted: to bury and hold in the dark this terrible grief.

Can you recall a time when your parents or guardians honored you? Released you to be who you were? What have your parents taught you about honoring your own soul and the souls of others?

I know the scripture verse for today says, "Obey your parents" (Ephesians 6:1) and "Honor your father and mother" (v. 2), and so we should, but where do we learn what that means? I cannot help but be moved to notice that my mother first honored me. She taught me in that moment that she released me to the barn and the world where I felt safest and most myself that obedience flows from honor. And honor isn't so much about following the rules as it is reverencing the person before you, acknowledging the one before you as holy ground, and acting accordingly.

Maybe I've had an easier time honoring my parents because they were willing to honor me in all the ways that I am unique and unrepeatable. Maybe it's much more difficult for you to honor your parents; maybe they haven't honored you. Maybe they didn't know how or couldn't for a whole host of reasons, reasons out of their control. Maybe they were simply repeating what they knew.

But it's never too late, even if they're gone. Can you imagine releasing them, honoring them for who they are and for giving you life?

READING: EPHESIANS 6:1–4

- Are there moments or wounds from childhood you'd like to address with your parents? If you can't share with them, consider sharing with someone close.
- How can you honor someone younger in your life? Maybe in the role as a mother, aunt, godmother, or friend.

◇

You are the light of the world.

Matthew 5:14

WEEK 43

FUMBLING ADVENTURES

Young Adulthood

It was August 1990, and I was driving through the Yukon in my little two-door hatchback on my way to Alaska. There I would attend graduate school for creative writing. I'd won a modest fellowship and was so excited I could barely think straight.

Though the road was rather dangerous, much of it unpaved, the route was spectacularly beautiful. It was hard not to get lost in the contemplation of God's majesty. The vastness and splendor—at every turn, a breathtaking vista. And somehow, me a witness to it.

I would drive for hours without seeing another vehicle. Along the way, I noticed signs that warned you to stop for gas because the next station was a hundred miles ahead—helpful things like that. At one point, nature called, and I pulled over to the side of the road and made my way into the woods. Just when I was situated for the rather vulnerable task at hand, I glanced up to see this sign—it read: *Do not stop here! Grizzlies feeding at salmon stream 100 feet ahead.*

The return to the hatchback was also—breathtaking.

I discovered that Tok, Alaska, where I spent the night in a youth hostel—a cot with a mosquito net thrown over it—was the sled-dog capital of the world. At one point, I heard a single woof, and in the next moment, every sled dog in the greater Tok vicinity was filling the night air with howls, enough to keep you awake all night long.

I look back on this adventure with gratitude and a hearty laugh at my own naïveté. When I finally made it into Anchorage, not having been eaten by a grizzly or tossed off the side of a mountain pass that was not paved, and without having slept, I was beyond relieved and grateful. That experience taught me that even more than successes, it's my mistakes, my failings, my occasionally unbelievably naïve moves that form me into the person I am and have tremendous value.

Jesus is interested in all of me, all of you. Yes, there are sins we need to confess and mistakes we need to correct if we can, but at no point does Jesus discard us because we try something and fail. Instead, He invites us into His perfection. He takes our fumblings and redeems them, bringing them into His plans for the kingdom.

I'm sure you can think of a few moments from your own life when a failing turned out to be a blessing, a teacher, even a gift. Or a moment when you were rescued by God from your own stupidity, and you gained a new understanding of His grace and kindness. Part of the "light" that is in us, is born out of our failures. Jesus can make it so.

In the Gospel for today, Christ is speaking directly to us. He said, "You are the light of the world" (Matthew 5:14). That can feel like a tremendously big call. We can find ourselves asking, *Lord, do You really mean me?*

But Jesus is incapable of making a misstatement, incapable of stretching the truth. He continued, "Let your light shine before others, so that they may see your good works and give glory to your Father in heaven" (v. 16). Our good works are not only our works of mercy— feeding the hungry, teaching the ignorant, visiting the imprisoned, sheltering the homeless, comforting the sorrowful—but the times when we dare to follow where He leads us, even into the Yukons of life in a hatchback. This becomes a good work when we give it to Jesus, when we give Him claim over us.

Every part of our lives can be claimed by Jesus and made glorious, can be assumed into the good works that give glory to the Father in Heaven. Dare to shine, sister. Pour all of your life into His redeeming love, withhold nothing, and let Him make you a living part of His glory.

READING: MATTHEW 5:14–16

- Where can you bless and release a painful memory of your journey, trusting it helped you become who you are today?
- Whom can you encourage on her path of embracing the call to become who God made her to be?

If you sow to the Spirit, you will reap eternal life from the Spirit. Galatians 6:8

WEEK 44
A SPACE OF MY OWN
Rite of Passage

I was about twenty-five and sitting in one of my sisters' kitchens. She was moving about, cleaning, cooking, and puttering. I remember this very distinct sense emanating from her: this was her home, her kingdom, and she was queen of this domain. It wasn't about power; rather, it was this deep sense of security, of being where she was supposed to be, doing what she was meant to be doing. She was rooted. In that moment, I realized just how much that sensibility was missing from my own life and how deeply I longed for it.

My husband and I married in our early fifties. Not long after that, we bought our house—a modest little venture on a dead-end street with a limited view of the lake behind us. It has two fireplaces, a large deck, a guest bedroom we have consecrated to the Blessed Mother—we call it the "Marian Suite." And my husband built a little shrine for the Holy Family in our backyard. We had our home blessed by my brother, a priest, on the Feast of the Sacred Heart, to which it is consecrated.

By far, my favorite feature is my prayer and writing room. My whole life I have wanted one room that would be reserved for prayer and writing—these two vocations that are so deeply linked in my life, like right and left lungs. They work together to let me inhale the Holy Spirit and exhale His encouragement onto the blank page. And at fifty-three, I finally have this room; it's consecrated to Our Lady at Prayer.

It has not been easy, waiting for this deep desire of my heart to come to fruition. On more than one occasion, I confess, I cried myself to sleep over a longing to have a place of my own. On more than one occasion I have raised my eyes to heaven and said, "Lord, I don't know how much longer I can go without this." I think a sense of home is a desire that has a particularly feminine strength and character, and the woman in me longed for it more than I can express.

But the Father had His reasons, I'm sure, for making me wait for so long. I have experienced a lifting in my spirit since settling in here. Consecrating our home to the Sacred Heart filled me with relief and deep joy. And it is clear to me that our home isn't simply an answer to my prayer and desire. Rather, "home" is a ministry all its own, and something to be shared with others. We want to find a way to make our homes places of hospitality and welcome, especially to those most in need. For my husband and me, we can also offer a hidden refuge, a retreat for those who need to come away and rest in our Marian suite.

One thing I've learned, sister, is that delay is not denial. Though heaven may be working out its plans more slowly than I would like, I can trust that the deep desires of my heart are known to the Father—because He placed them there. He created them within me. When they are not being fulfilled, I can have confidence that He is at work in me, accomplishing something for my good, purifying me in such a way that when my desire is fulfilled—maybe in a way I couldn't possibly imagine—it will be all the sweeter and richer.

Never be afraid of your deepest desires. Never be ashamed of them. Go ahead and name them; claim them as given to you by your

Father. What are they? To get married, or have a baby? Healing for you or someone you love? To have a good friend? To find meaningful work that makes your soul sing?

We want to tend to our desires with great intentionality—that is, to "sow to the Spirit," as Saint Paul said in today's reading (Galatians 6:8). I wonder if my home would be as consecrated as it is if I had not learned this lesson beforehand. When our deepest longings are slow to be fulfilled, we can be tempted to settle for something less than what the Father has in mind for us, to sow to the flesh by taking the easy route rather than the right one.

Let the Father take your desire and lift it into eternity. The joy that follows is not of this world.

READING: GALATIANS 6:7–8

- Has completing a degree, home ownership, or a relationship you're longing for felt elusive? What would "sowing" that desire to the Holy Spirit look like?
- Are you witnessing a loved one undergoing a delay in her next step in life? How can you support her?

"Seek me with all your heart."

WEEK 45
MY FATHER'S CONFIDENCE
School

To a large degree, I owe my vocation as a writer to my father. I was just out of college and contemplating graduate school in creative writing or law school. My father was an attorney and then sat on the bench as a judge for almost twenty years. I have two siblings who practice law and numerous siblings who are married to attorneys or those working in law in some form or another. Law was big at my house growing up—and I admired and appreciated that world.

I lamented to my father about the difficulty of choosing a life path: Law was engaging and worthy, and I could probably support myself; writing was worthy too, but do people even read anymore? How could I make it a profession? He was patient as I swung fitfully back and forth, weighing and wondering, filled with angst.

But then he said this: "Of all my children, I think you would make a very good lawyer. You love to reason, and you would be very good at making an argument." I thought he might be finished, but then he continued. "But when you write," he said, pausing a moment to search for the right expression, "I don't even know where that comes from." His voice carried something in it like reverence, something like amazement, a touch of paternal pride. "It seems to me," he went on, "that that is something very special."

I'll never forget that moment and being flooded with—not just permission, but a reverent kind of encouragement—to be exactly who I was created to be. In that moment, I recognized that my writing was a calling, not a dalliance. It needed to be taken seriously, to be cultivated and nourished. It had import and purpose.

Furthermore, my father's confidence in the fact that I had been given something special, despite the fact this specialness set me apart from my father—I would pursue a plan very different from his own— was more freeing than I can express. He trusted in God's plans for my flourishing, and he understood that meant something far more important than making money or taking the safest road possible.

The words from Jeremiah for today's reflection sing in my soul. I believe in them so deeply, for me—and for you, sister. "For surely I know the plans I have for you. . . . If you seek me with all your heart, I will let you find me, says the LORD" (Jeremiah 29:11, 13–14).

Writing has been my way to find God; it has been my prayer and my breath and more satisfying than I could possibly imagine. It has bridged me with a world of people I would otherwise never have connected with and has softened my heart with its demands for discipline, editing, and revision. God brings humble projects to my door, and I take them into my little prayer and writing room and love them into existence to the best of my ability.

We can have great confidence that the Father has plans for us, that He desires our collaboration in building up the kingdom, and what's more, that this collaboration will bring us the deepest satisfaction that there is. Everyone gets an assignment; everyone has a critical part to play. It may or may not involve renown or financial security—but it will cause us to flourish in Him and to become more and more ourselves.

When I find myself far from flourishing, I have to wonder if I have strayed from the plan, or rejected the plan, or if I'm trying to be something I'm not. I know at those times I have to get back to seeking Him with my whole heart and waiting for Him to find me once again.

How are you doing? Are you flourishing? Are you seeking Him with all your heart? Are you leaning into your charisms, developing them, stewarding them, and then giving them back to the Lord to put to good work in the kingdom?

Trust in the Father's plan; trust that it is His ardent desire that you flourish. Nothing less. And if you're a little low on trust, that's all right. You can borrow Jeremiah's and mine.

READING: JEREMIAH 29:11–14

- Are you in a place where you have discerned a plan for pursuing education? Take a deep breath and trust with confidence in the plan that God has for you.
- If you find yourself on an unexpected path, take the time to bring this to the Lord in prayer, to either praise Him in thanksgiving or to probe Him for what is next for you.

The real widow, left alone, has set her hope on God. 1 Timothy 5:5

WEEK 46

A LEGACY OF

BITTERNESS

Family of Origin

My grandmother and I share a birthday, something you might think would bond us. But we were never close. My mother and my paternal grandmother experienced deep tension that took a toll on the whole family, especially my mother.

Grandma's life was difficult. Her husband died after a protracted illness leaving her with six small children to raise alone. I have often wondered if some of the meanness that spilled out on my mom was just Grandma's loneliness coming out sideways.

As my grandmother aged, her faculties began to fail. She lived alone in the same house where my father grew up, in a small country town. All of her children had moved many hours away.

One day when I was ten, she called my mother. Mom listened quietly and after a minute said, "It's okay, Grandma. We'll be there as soon as we can." Right away, Mom and I were driving across the winter fields on our way to Grandma's.

When we arrived, we knew something was wrong. The house smelled foul, and Grandma was agitated. Stepping into the house, we understood the smell was coming from used diapers that were everywhere. Mom gave me some garbage bags and rubber gloves and set me to cleaning while she ran Grandma a bath. I will never forget watching my mother bathe my grandmother, wash her hair, and help her get dried and dressed.

In that moment, I knew: my mother was an absolute genius, and this was a triumph in mercy and compassion.

I wonder if I could have, would have, done the same. How about you? It's very easy to say, "Not my problem," and go on about my business, especially when it comes to the needs of someone who has hurt me. Though my mother would have been justified in tossing this task to a sister-in-law, she didn't. Grandma called her, and she responded with such gentleness.

I see, of course, this is what Jesus does for me. He provides for me. Period. It doesn't matter that I fail, that I sin, that I carry an old bitterness or resentment around with me like a sack of wet cement. When I call, I find He's already on His way to me. He provides, just like my mother provided for my grandmother, with tenderness, generosity, and without the severe judgments I probably deserve.

As I grow older, I hope that I'm losing the "tally mentality," that interior way of keeping score with others, always on the ready to measure someone's worthiness in my own eyes. Rather, I hope I'm becoming more like my mom, responding to the real need before me without asking questions like, "Does she deserve it?"

Perhaps we'd love more quickly if we knew other people's stories, or we understood that they were deserving of love regardless. Saint Paul was getting at this when he said, "Whoever does not provide for relatives, and especially for family members, has denied the faith and is worse than an unbeliever" (1 Timothy 5:8). The extraordinary emphasis he places on caring for our loved ones cannot be overlooked.

There is no mention of whether they are worthy, doting, faithful, loving—only that we are to provide for their needs.

And I have to believe that he doesn't simply mean material needs. More than any material help we might have provided that day, I know it was my mother's gentleness that must have made the angels sing. And surely that is Paul's chief concern, that we provide not just material goods, but relationship, that we give not only of our resources but of ourselves, our time, our care, our listening and tending.

I find it helpful sometimes to take a "care" inventory with regards to those I love. Am I spending time with them, listening to them, attending to them, just like my mom cared for my grandmother that day? Am I providing for them beyond the material, offering forgiveness easily and generously where it is needed?

Are there people in your life right now who need you? You, and not your resources. People who need you to listen or to help or to spend a little extra time with them? Let's aim for that together, sister, making heaven sing with our kindness.

READING: 1 TIMOTHY 5:5–8

- Have you seen transformation in the people in your life that gives you greater insight into your own story?
- If you are struggling with caring for members of your family, ask the Lord to shine a light on healthy boundaries.

Let your gentleness be known. Philippians 4:5

HOLDING SACRED SPACE

Friendship

A dear friend came to visit. She brought a few chapters from her life story to share. She was writing this autobiography mainly for herself, and a bit for her children and a few close friends. I was honored to be included in that last group.

With a hot cup of tea, she settled into my couch with a blanket and a box of tissues at her feet and turned to page one. Then she read slowly, beautifully, for an hour or so while another dear friend and I listened. Her life unfolded before us, lovely yet painful. We sat quietly and witnessed the earliest days of her life and some of the staggering tragedies that set her on her way—into trauma and childhood rape, an abusive marriage, and an abortion.

My friend and I simply listened, an hour or two one day, an hour or two the next. She just read and occasionally paused to cry or to take a deep breath before continuing. A striking theme rose to the surface: over her journey, she had no one to talk to, no one to listen, no one who understood.

A few days later, as I drove her to the airport for her trip home, she said, "I'm leaving here a changed woman." I could hear it in her voice. She sounded more free, lighter, more comfortable in her own skin. She continued, "I think I just needed someone to hear all of that and to still love me. I just needed to come out of hiding and to completely be myself."

And the message to me in this could not be plainer: listening is healing. We offered no feedback, no commentary, no advice. We didn't try to fix anything or change her. We didn't dare say, "Don't feel bad." Instead, we quietly cried with her.

In my youth, I know I was a "trampler." How often I trampled on the soul of another by trying to "help," or to "fix it," or to offer advice. How often I marched through the story of another soul as though I were a general in charge of an invading army, rather than sit quietly and simply receive that person's experience as the sacred gift it was. How often do my friends come to me—not looking for advice or answers—but with the deep soul-need of simply being heard?

It's worth asking for all of us: Am I a good listener? Or am I a "trampler," even when I don't mean to be? Does someone in my life need my listening presence right now?

I think sometimes we imagine that compassion should be noticeable or dramatic when more often than not, to be effective, it must be quiet, hidden, virtually invisible to all but the person who is receiving it—and cloaked in gentleness. The person who listens possesses a kind of reverence, a divine tenderness that somehow joins in the holy work that the Lord does for us in Adoration of the Blessed Sacrament: He listens.

We've lost a bit of our respect for gentleness in a culture that values aggressiveness and lauds the extrovert. It's almost seen as a weakness, something to be medicated or corrected with assertiveness training. But even two thousand years ago, Saint Paul understood that gentleness is a gateway to peace and joy.

Today's reading is taken from his letter to the Philippians, which is often referred to as the "epistle of joy." And in it, he touched on some of the most important features of Christian friendship. He wrote, "Let your gentleness be known to everyone. . . . And the peace of God, which surpasses all understanding, will guard your hearts and your minds in Christ Jesus" (Philippians 4:5, 7).

In my experience I see that gentleness breeds peace and gratitude; it creates space for authenticity—and how wildly our culture needs permission to be authentic.

Saint Paul reminds us that the Lord is near. Let's rest in the arms of that truth. He is near—through you, through me, through our listening and receiving our loved ones. When He's near, we can simply sit and be available, and let the Lord do the heavy lifting.

READING: PHILIPPIANS 4:4–7

- If you tend to be a "trampler," resolve to take an example from this week's story and listen with your whole being.
- Examine gently how you can seek authentic friendship with like-minded women. Invite Jesus in to help you become the friend you would like to be.

✧

"Your sins are forgiven." Mark 2:5

LOOKING PAST
THE TOADS

Romantic Relationship

When I was younger, I was pretty insecure, and the men I seemed to fall in with were somewhat—shall we say—amphibious.

One dude called me up half an hour before we were to meet to tell me he had to cancel our date because he was hungover. Delightful. The "devout Catholic" fellow told me after some months of dating that he just wasn't attracted to me, except in certain light. Terrific. There were active alcoholics, aimless loafers, and even one not-so-ex ex-convict. (I still don't know what happened to my wallet.) Real toads that stayed toads long after they'd been kissed. It's a common thread for the women I know: we settle for so little.

But then I met my husband. Right away, his care and tenderness for me made me feel cherished right down to my toes.

Once, when I had to have surgery on my face and the follow-up care took some attention, he set to the task with both military precision and the gentleness of the Good Shepherd. Icing was particularly important and had to be done regularly—he kept track with his stopwatch. Even post-op, his care was so noticeable that the nurses commented on it. When he left me to bring the car around, they surrounded my wheelchair saying, "We know when someone is going to be well-cared for or not when they return home. You are going to receive exquisite care." They were right.

From hungover toads—to exquisite care! If you haven't already, you can make the transition.

The lessons I learned from our culture about romance took some undoing. The false notions about how attractive I needed to be in order to be worthy of being loved were deeply entrenched. Those lies were the most pernicious and took the most time to be extracted from my heart.

But the Father is a patient, gentle teacher. Slowly He taught me to honor myself in romantic relationships and to trust that I was worthy of being well-cared-for. And that caring for me with tenderness is good for the soul of my beloved too. The grace goes both ways.

It took me some time to realize that the Father would never ask me to settle for a toad. He wants to see His daughter with a champion! Someone who will know she is a heavenly gift to be supported, nurtured, and treasured. And to know that the most attractive thing about her is the gorgeous soul the Father gave her. A man worthy of her would know that.

It took being well-loved and cherished—down to my toes—to learn that romantic relationships were to teach me something about how wildly the Lord loves me, about how He would go even to the cross, to heal me, to keep me safe, to see me flourish.

Today's scripture reflection illustrates this idea so vividly. Jesus is surrounded by the crowds, and there's no way to reach him, so "when they could not bring him to Jesus because of the crowd, they removed the roof above him. . . . They let down the mat on which the paralytic lay" (Mark 2:4).

Can you imagine yourself as the paralyzed soul, lying there, longing to be healed by Jesus and having no way through to Him? Who would do whatever it took to get you to Jesus? Who would take charge of your need, get creative, and execute a plan to get you to your Healer?

Though this illustration from the Bible is focusing on friendship, I find it applies perfectly to my marriage. That's what romantic relationships are meant to teach us: to show us how to cherish one another and to bring one another into flourishing in Christ. I want to be the kind of spouse to get my husband to heaven, to bring him nearer to Jesus through the strength of my prayers, gentleness, and support. And if it called for it, to crash through the roof.

I didn't marry my husband until I was fifty-two, so if you're still waiting for your beloved, be patient and don't you dare settle for a toad.

READING: MARK 2:2–5

- When you pray about the painful and hilarious memories of past dates, ask the Lord for healing.
- Consider if you could better meet your loved one's needs or if you could communicate your own needs more clearly.

"What will it profit them if they gain the whole world but forfeit their life?" Matthew 16:26

PRICKED BY
CONSCIENCE

Workplace

I'd been working several years at a prestigious institution when I was asked to do work that was directly in opposition to Catholic teaching. I panicked. I knew I couldn't do the work, but what if I got fired? Lost my income? I wasn't the least bit composed. Imagine a squawking chicken running pell-mell.

Things got hairy. Human Resources told me that if I did not perform the work, I would be fired. A Catholic lawyer in the area gave me the number of a civil rights attorney. He told me how the law protected me and gave me the exact verbiage to use. When Human Resources made another uncomfortable visit, I was better prepared.

It was Ash Wednesday. A lovely woman from H. R. came to clarify my objections.

"I'm Catholic," I said. "I can't do this work for religious reasons."

"I see," she said, and then she caught sight of the ashes on my forehead. "It's Ash Wednesday," she said quietly. Her gaze fell to the floor. "I'm such a bad Catholic."

It turns out the law was on my side—I could not be fired, but I could almost hear my IQ clunk as it hit the basement floor in the eyes of my colleagues.

One day, there was a knock on my door. A man I'd been working with for several years came in and said, "I just wanted to thank you for what you did." I was stunned. He continued, "I didn't want to do that work either, and I didn't know that, legally, I didn't have to."

So much grace to glean from this little episode in my life. So much gratitude sprang up as a result, completely leveling the anxiety I had had while living through it. And how I learned. Three things stand out from the incident.

One, you can do the right thing and feel crazy-scared. Even Jesus in the Agony in the Garden felt such dread that He sweat tears of blood, so a few sleepless nights of worry on my part, a few agonized fits of venting on the phone don't disqualify me from doing what is right.

Two, you can do the right thing and do it awkwardly, but still do the right thing. Jesus never tells us that we are disqualified from the kingdom for lacking poise or eloquence. Those attributes might make us feel better or more admirable, but they are not required.

Three, you simply never know how your little act of obedience is going to light a fire in the soul of another. You never know how even the tiniest act of faith is going to lift someone else into righteousness and put them on a holier path. You can never underestimate how Jesus will take our minuscule efforts at righteousness and magnify them to build up His kingdom.

Are you struggling to do the right thing? In some little or great matter? Are you faced with a decision that may disrupt your sense of safety, personally or professionally? I know how frightening it can be; so do all of the saints. You're in good company if you are doing battle for the good, the true, and the beautiful. You are not alone—the Church stands with you. Receive strength from her.

Take heart and rest in the scripture reading for today, when Jesus tells us, "For the Son of Man is to come with his angels in the glory of his Father, and then he will repay everyone for what has been done" (Matthew 16:27). Sister, nothing is worth your soul. No worldly gain is more satisfying than doing God's will and upholding His truth. You become a blazing lamp unto the feet of your brothers and sisters in Christ, even those with little faith at all. And think of the joy your fidelity will bring to the Sacred Heart of Jesus and the multitudes in heaven.

And in my experience, Jesus is so often quick to repay us for our faithfulness. He gives us a taste of His joy here on earth.

In my next, current job, my office hovers over the chapel where students hold Adoration of the Blessed Sacrament each Monday. Jesus, literally beneath my feet all day, holds me up so I can uphold Him.

READING: MATTHEW 16:26–27

- Have you felt challenged in your workplace because of your faith? Take any stress to the Lord in prayer.
- If coworkers or colleagues have made fun of your faith, how have you felt? If you've witnessed it, what have you done to help someone feel supported in living her faith in the world?

◇

"Do you love me?" John 21:17

WEEK 50

HEALING EVEN
IN DARKNESS

Church Community

J o" is an impressive woman. Faithful and highly respected in a challenging medical field. When we first started meeting for spiritual direction, she was poised and articulate, but I could see there was something brewing under her polished comportment. Over several months, the story began to unfold.

When she was just a child, preparing for her First Holy Communion, she was molested by her priest. A few days later, she had to receive her First Communion from the very same man that had betrayed her so heartlessly. The damage that was done was unspeakably deep. It placed a wedge between Jo and the Blessed Sacrament, between her and her own body and sexuality, and between her and the Church that she wanted to believe in and trust with all her heart.

As we worked through this trauma—she was also seeking help from a therapist who specialized in this field—I stood witness to a very slow-moving healing. Eventually, bravely, Jo gave her permission to be prayed over by a priest—also a specialist in this area. I was there as he and his healing team prayed ancient and powerful prayers of the Church over Jo, covering her anew with the protection of the angels and saints and the Blood of Jesus, casting out this trauma that had oppressed her for so long.

And though she's still on the road to healing and battling every day for her faith, I stand in awe that she would find the strength to place her trust in the Church and in one of her shepherds.

It is an exceptionally difficult reality to accept that corruption exists in our Church. That for every Saint Peter, James, John, Andrew, Phillip, Mary, Elizabeth, and Magdalene, there is also a Judas. It's disconcerting to realize that corruption walks among us; it is not far off but close enough to touch. It sits with us at table and shares a meal.

But, slowly and surely, Jo is teaching me: there can be forgiveness, healing, and reconciliation—no matter how wicked the wound. In Jo's case, her abuser is long since deceased. Still, she has found a way to come out of isolation and to make her voice heard, and to make peace with her abuser and those who protected him from repercussions. She is choosing forgiveness.

Has the Church, or one of her members, failed you? Harmed you? Driven you from her? You may be completely justified in your anger or distrust, but can you also turn to Jesus, like Jo, and ask Him to be with you in that betrayal? He is an expert in this pain, having been so betrayed Himself. He knows this wound better than anyone and longs to heal and free you from it.

In today's passage from the Gospel of John, when Jesus asked Peter repeatedly, "Do you love me?" it's almost as if the Lord wanted to remind Peter of this painful reality—that the Church and her members will fail you sometimes, just like Peter denied Christ three times during His passion.

"Jesus said to Simon Peter, 'Simon son of John, do you love me more than these?' He said to him, 'Yes, Lord; you know that I love you.' Jesus said to him, 'Feed my lambs'" (John 21:15).

Jesus went, asking the flummoxed Peter, "Do you love me?" You can feel the tension growing. "Peter felt hurt because he said to him the third time, 'Do you love me?' And he said to him, 'Lord, you know everything; you know that I love you.' Jesus said to him, 'Feed my sheep'" (v. 17).

Jesus did not minimize Peter's failing, but neither did He abandon him in his weakness. Instead, He forgave Peter, gave him an opportunity to atone for his failing, and then He gave him a mission.

When I have been wounded, I want to remember that this potential for failure lives in me too, the little and great ways I want to cut corners on ethics, the little and great ways I want to live in just a little more comfort and a little less virtue. I want to remember that Jesus knew Judas, He broke bread with him, even as Judas broke His heart. We can tap into that same radical forgiveness, grace, and healing for the wounds we receive—and sometimes give—even within our church family.

READING: JOHN 21:15–17

- Have you experienced any wounds being part of a church community?
- What mission do you feel you've received as a member of the Mystical Body of Christ, the Church?

I can do all
things
through him.

Philippians 4:13

A MORE ABUNDANT LIFE

Relationship with the Lord

The doctors first suspected I might have something wrong with me in my twenties. Lots of weird neurological symptoms, vertigo, tingling, and something just not quite right when I walked. A barrage of expensive tests came back normal. So I bumbled on for the next two decades, occasionally having flare-ups of "weirdness" while certain folks just assumed I was a hypochondriac.

Then, finally, at age forty-one, I went blind in one eye: a very characteristic, first symptom of multiple sclerosis. My uncle had MS, and he was in a wheelchair by about forty, so I took a deep breath and prepared myself for life to get very, very small.

But that's not what happened. Not even close. In fact, I have never been so productive as since I received my diagnosis. I've written six more books and traveled the United States giving retreats and talks. My monthly column, "Your Heart, His Home," has been picked up around the country. I've traveled abroad many times, including a pilgrimage to the Holy Land. I've become an aunt and great-aunt, and a godmother on several happy occasions. I've hiked through the mountains in Wyoming and taken a dip in the Sea of Galilee. I've been certified as a spiritual director, resulting in hours of incredible conversations with precious souls. I married a spectacular Italian and bought a little house, creating a room just for prayer and writing, a lifelong dream of mine. Life is full, more focused, but not small at all.

It's true, I'm tired all the time. I sleep more than the average person my age. I can't feel my feet properly, and I'm clumsier than I used to be, but I find it almost hilarious that God decided to make me more productive, to give my voice a greater reach in the world despite these limitations. Illness is no obstacle to God in making me effective in His kingdom, like virginity was no obstacle to the Incarnation nor death an obstacle to the return of Lazarus.

I was sure that my future would be a burden to those I loved the most. Instead, I get letters from readers who say my books have changed their lives and a husband who loves me more than any other human being has ever loved me.

I wonder sometimes about what Saint Paul is teaching us in this passage to the Philippians in today's scripture from prison. Maybe it isn't so much about whether we have or have not, but a reminder to stay focused—not on our circumstances but on the Giver of all good gifts. He wrote, "I can do all things through him who strengthens me" (Philippians 4:13). I want to measure my success by Paul's standards: the Lord's will and my cooperation and collaboration with it. Whether that be prison or paradise, in love or loneliness, in sickness or health. The only obstacle to becoming effective in God's kingdom is me.

If I'm not being effective, I have to ask: Where's my focus? Where am I putting what limited energy I have? MS has been a gift in that it keeps me completely dependent on God for everything—energy, creativity, opportunities, money to pay the medical bills. So much non-essential kerfuffle has fallen away. I see God using this condition to help me get razor-sharp about serving Him, making every moment count.

Paul made every moment count, even in prison! How are you doing at making every moment count? What are some of the obstacles you face that make you feel incapable? Can you give them to the Lord? Can you lean on Him just a bit more and ask Him to strengthen you and to make up for anything you lack?

Remember, Paul stayed true to his mission—it hadn't changed because he was in prison. The Father is not fickle in His mission for you or me either. He has a mission for us, and it cannot be robbed by our circumstances. In my Father's economy, there's enough money, enough creativity, enough time. More than enough.

In Christ who is my strength, I am enough. And so are you, sister. Let Him prove it to you.

READING: PHILIPPIANS 4:12–13

- What challenge has brought you to your knees, questioning your relationship with God as one of true care? Bring this to Him in prayer today.
- Do you measure your gifts by God's standards of surrender to His will for your life, letting Him be your strength? What do you need to recalibrate in light of this today?

Everything has become new! 2 Corinthians 5:17

WEEK 52

MADE NEW

by Jenna Guizar

What a beautiful journey this has been, this unraveling of our identities to then be formed and made new by Our Lord. He is such a patient Father, taking us by the hand, walking us step by step deeper into a relationship with Him.

I hope you have experienced growth over these past fifty-two weeks, even if it feels small. I hope you have witnessed the Lord plant new seeds in you that He desires to continue to water and see take root. He will do it, with His gentle hand and His mighty love.

You've come this far, dear sister. He has even more in store for you: His unending mercy and magnificent love. Our reception of these will continue to breathe freedom into our very bones. He will continue to grow you and me, day in and day out, moment by moment, if only we give way to His grace, if only we continue to surrender.

You are a beloved daughter of the Father, and I hope and pray you never, ever forget it. And if you do, as sometimes the world can diminish our assurance in Our Father's heart, come back. Come back to your rootedness in His love. Come again to this book, to these truths, to Our Lord who whispers again and again: *I am here.*

READING: 2 CORINTHIANS 5:15–19

- In what ways are you made new after this year of reflection and prayer on your identity?
- The Lord desires you to know your truest identity as God's beloved daughter. Who do you want to share this truth with today who may need this reminder?

Find out more about Blessed is She and
our writers at blessedisshe.net.

ABOUT THE AUTHORS

Leana Bowler is a wife and mama of six little ones. She is a Holy Rosary enthusiast who loves chapel veils and the joy of the gospel. She enjoys the miracles of family life, strong coffee, good books, Arizona sunsets, and encountering others on this journey to sainthood.

Brittany Calavitta is an enthusiastic advocate for a good book, strong coffee, and a hopeful heart. After battling years of infertility, she and her husband welcomed their first child on September 11, 2016. While balancing time between life with a preschooler and a husband who travels for ministry, Brittany dances professionally all over Southern California, where her family currently resides. She is a contributing author to *Here Too: Where We Find God*.

Jenna Guizar is a wife and mama in sunny Arizona. She loves spending time with her barber husband, her four daughters, and their son. After falling in love with the Lord through deep, faithful friends who prayed and spoke hope into her life, Jenna founded Blessed is She, which became her mission ground to help women fall more in love with the Lord and into deeper friendships with one another.

Liz Kelly is an award-winning speaker and the author of nine books, including *Jesus Approaches: What Contemporary Women Can Learn About Healing, Freedom & Joy from the Women of the New Testament* which has won a number of awards, including Best Book, 2019, Religion Category, Best Book Awards. She holds advanced degrees in creative writing and Catholic studies. She is trained as a spiritual director in the Ignatian exercises and leads retreats with a particular focus on helping women to flourish in their faith. She teaches in Catholic Studies at the University of Saint Thomas (MN) and serves as managing editor for *Logos: A Journal of Catholic Thought and Culture.*

Nell O'Leary is the managing editor for Blessed is She. She is also an attorney-turned-writer, speaker, and editor while tending to her husband and five kiddos. She also facilitates Blessed is She community groups around the world as she loves helping women find sisterhood. Her undergrad is in English from University of Minnesota and her JD from Ave Maria School of Law. Notably, she can down a hot cocoa in two seconds.

Susanna Spencer holds a master's in theology from the Franciscan University of Steubenville and is the theological editor of Blessed is She. She lives with her philosopher husband and four kids in Saint Paul, Minnesota. She loves reading theology, attending beautiful liturgies, cooking delicious food, and casually following baseball. She is the narrator for *Rise Up: Shining with Virtue* and *Maranatha: The Story of Our Savior.*